Ricky Martin

RED-HOT AND ON THE RISE!

KATHLEEN TRACY

Zebra Books
Kensington Publishing Corp.
http://www.zebrabooks.com

ZEBRA BOOKS are published by

Kensington Publishing Corp.
850 Third Avenue
New York, NY 10022

First Printing: July, 1999
10 9 8 7 6 5 4 3

Printed in the United States of America

TABLE OF CONTENTS

Acknowledgments 7
Introduction 9
1. A Star Is Born 11
2. Getting into Menudo 21
3. Leaving Menudo 33
4. A New Career 43
5. Going Solo 51
6. Checking into *General Hospital* 61
7. Climbing the Charts 71
8. Debuting on Broadway 81
9. Back in the Recording Studio 89
10. On Tour 97
11. Ricky Style! 107
12. The Latin King of Pop 117
13. Today's Latin Music Scene 127
14. The Grammys 137
15. America's New Pop Star 147
16. Still Ricky 157
Ricky Fast Facts 161
Ricky on the 'Net 164
Filmography 169
Discography 170

Acknowledgments

The author would like to thank my agent, Robert Di-Forio, and my editor, John Scognamiglio. The former for going above and beyond the call with his tireless efforts on my behalf; the latter for trusting me to get this book done on time and for believing it was the right book on the right man at the right time.

Introduction

He's only twenty-seven, but Ricky Martin has already lived a fuller, more adventurous life than most people do in a lifetime. Before he was old enough to drive, he had performed in front of literally millions of fans as part of an internationally famous singing group; he has known the ecstasy of living out a childhood fantasy and the fear and vulnerability of being a potential has-been before he was old enough to legally buy himself a drink. But instead of falling victim to his own early success, Ricky reinvented himself as an actor and solo artist who now commands the loyalty and adoration of fans the world over.

If there ever was a truly international star, it is Ricky Martin, and now this musical sensation is poised to conquer the United States with the release of his first English-language album. And that sound you hear is the bursting of bubble gum and the snapping of rock guitar strings as they give way to the sensual, infectious beat of Ricky's Latin rhythms that will soon have America joyfully dancing to a salsa beat.

1

A Star Is Born

When you think of Puerto Rico, images of balmy beaches and warm breezes lazily drift into your mind's eye. But if you listen carefully, you'll also hear a distinctive backbeat, an earthy rhythm that has your shoulders moving and your body swaying almost before you're aware of it. But to Puerto Ricans, music is more than just sounds to listen to; it's an expression of who they are as a people.

''As you know, Puerto Ricans are very musical people,'' says Ricky. ''They say that babies are born with a sense of rhythm in Puerto Rico. Music is a part of life there. There's no school where you can go and learn it. It's just a question of feeling it. We look for any excuse to create music—with a spoon, with your fingers, with a pen, with anything. It's just, Let's have fun!

''When we talk about music in Puerto Rico, we have a little bit of everything,'' he explains. ''We are influenced by Latin America, Europe, Africa, and, of course, the United States. Because of that, we try to keep our roots and we go to the African rhythms.''

The island of Puerto Rico was among the first areas to be settled after Christopher Columbus discovered the New World in the late 1400s. Small but beautiful, with mountains covering over half the island, the island is home to both lush rain forests and, on the southwestern corner of the island, desert, and its coastal beaches are among the most sparkling in all the Caribbean, Ricky's favorite being Palominito, located on the northeast side of Puerto Rico.

Ricky grew up in awe of the nature surrounding him. He loved the rain forests, where over *one hundred billion* gallons of rain fall every year, and as a boy he would try to find tiny coqui frogs—named because of their cricketlike chirp—that abound on the island but are found nowhere else in the world but Puerto Rico. As far as Ricky is concerned, his native home offers everything he could want. "Beautiful women, beautiful beaches, great food, great hotels, beautiful rain forest, beautiful weather . . . I don't know, what else?

"Puerto Rico is more than where I'm from," Ricky says. "Puerto Rico is my life. Puerto Rico is my beginning."

Enrique Martin Morales was born in the Hato Rey district of San Juan on Christmas Eve, 1971, "a very boring date," he jokes. Nicknamed Kiki—"It's short for Enrique."—Ricky got his first taste of what fate had in store for him when he won a baby beauty contest.

Although his parents, Enrique and Nerieda, divorced when Ricky was still a youngster, he considers his middle-class upbringing a normal one.

"My childhood was very healthy," he says, adding that despite being from a broken home, he was very close "to both my parents. I did whatever I wanted. If I wanted to be with my mother, I lived with her, and the same with my father: if I wanted to be with him, I stayed where he was. I loved them both very much. And although they were no longer married, they were very good friends.

"My family life was very peaceful when I was young, and my family was very close." Ricky's extended family was also large, with five half siblings, "two from my mother, and three from my father. But I am the only one of my parents' marriage." Raised Catholic, Ricky attended parochial schools, and while perhaps not *the* most popular kid in class, he had plenty of friends. But unlike other children his age, Ricky had interests beyond the usual childhood pursuits. Instead of wishing for a ball and bat or pining after a new bicycle, Ricky yearned to perform, a desire that both his mother and father encouraged and supported.

Ricky's interest in movies and music was obvious from the time he could talk. One of his earliest memories is of going to see *Star Wars* when he was just six years old.

"It was amazing," he remembers, saying that the films of the *Star Wars* trilogy are among his favorite movies of all time, with *Return of the Jedi* being his favorite of the first three *Star Wars* films. "Jabba the Hutt was amazing. I love that disgusting bastard; he was so ugly and disgusting, but he affected me some way, somehow, you know. Not that it's my role model." Ricky laughs, saying that that honor went to Luke Skywalker.

"I *was* Luke Skywalker. Every time we played, I was Luke Skywalker. *Nobody* else could be Luke Skywalker."

Music was also a primary force in young Ricky's life, but he says that was to be expected. "Being born in

Puerto Rico—yes, that makes us very passionate toward music.''

Ironically, though, when he was growing up, Ricky was drawn more to American pop music—particularly bands like Journey, Boston, and Foreigner, as well as performers like David Bowie—than he was to the sensual sounds of his own homeland, which is why the first album he ever bought was the soundtrack to *Saturday Night Fever.* Yes, it's true: Ricky Martin was a Bee Gees fanatic, with one of his favorite cuts from the album being ''How Deep Is Your Love?''

''I was, like, seven, but I thought I was John Travolta.'' Martin laughs. ''I was, like, combing my hair back and walking with a little limp like him, and I wanted to wear polyester, and my mom was like, 'This is Puerto Rico, it's really hot, you're not wearing it!' I'd be screaming, 'There are no sizes for me.' I was so bad. I was really wild, but it was a phase, because I was always into rock.

''I was really influenced by rock music because of my brothers. Then one day my mom had had enough. She told me and my two older brothers, 'Enough with rock! I cannot stand it anymore!' ''

It wasn't so much that Nerieda didn't want her sons to listen to rock and roll; it was more that she didn't want them to ignore the music of their own culture because of it. She wanted them to appreciate Latin culture and music as much as they did America's. It was important her sons be as well versed in Latin genres such as *cumbia,* a type of indigenous Columbian music and dance style, as they were in Top 40 tunes.

''She asked us, 'Do you know about Latin sounds?' '' Ricky recalls. ''We were like, 'Duh . . . no. It's not cool;

we want rock.'" Nerieda gave Ricky and his brothers a crash course on Latin music history, dragging them to concerts by such legendary performers as Celia Cruz and Tito Puente.

"She told us, 'This is music that you have to learn to appreciate because this is you, it's where you come from, this is your sound.' " Ricky admits that he wasn't "too happy at the concert," but says he eventually did open his ears and heart to the sounds his mother wanted him to hear. Now, of course, he can't thank his mother enough for making him expand his musical horizons.

"Not just because I can talk about this music, but because I can perform it too." Even though Ricky isn't really a salsa performer, he does incorporate the Latin rhythms with his rock-and-roll sensibility to create his unique sound. "I can play with all these sounds and I'm comfortable with it—so, Mom, thank you so much."

But as a child, Ricky didn't fantasize about being the musical performer he would eventually become. Instead, his interests were geared more toward acting. As a child, Ricky was always the ham of the family, never missing an opportunity to have his picture taken or be the center of attention at family gatherings. He also participated in his church choir and in school plays. But his ambitions went far beyond his parents' living rooms and the church and school walls.

"When I was six years old, I said to my father, 'Daddy, I want to be an artist,' " Ricky remembers. "Well, he didn't know what hit him, of course. 'Where did you get that idea?' But he also said, 'If you want to become an artist, how can we get you there?' He was like, 'Really, how can I help you?' "

But by that time Ricky was already taking singing and dancing lessons, and although neither parent was involved in the arts—his dad was a psychologist and his mom worked as an accountant—they let Ricky pursue performing.

"For sure! They don't have anything to do with show-business, but they wanted to give their son everything he wanted, so they immediately thought, 'How can we help?' 'No problem, I'll handle it,' I said, as opinionated six-year-olds do. But it was my father who arranged my first audition for a television commercial. My dad took me to a modeling agency. At age seven I did my first commercial for TV and kept doing that for a while."

While they knew performing was their son's full-time passion, neither of Ricky's parents really believed it would become a full-time profession.

"My parents were very supportive, but they weren't the typical stage parents. For my first audition I went by myself, riding my bike. When I came back home, I announced that I was leaving to be an entertainer. I was eleven years old at the time. They started laughing, and then they started crying."

Ricky wasn't really leaving home for good, just to shoot a soda commercial. "After that, I did some theater, too." Despite finding work in commercials and theater, Ricky wasn't really satisfied. Nor would he be until he fulfilled his true dream, one that seemed impossible to those around him. What Ricky wanted more than anything was to join the singing group Menudo, which had burst onto the Latin music scene in the summer of 1978. The original members were Johnny Lozada, Ricky Melendez,

Ray Reyes, Miguel Cancel, Charlie Masso, and Rene Farraet.

"They were very successful," Ricky says. "I had been a fan of the group since it began in 1977. I was always stubbornly determined to be one of them. That became my next project: How can I get into that group?"

However, the impetus wasn't so much performing. "I didn't want to be a singer, not then," Ricky admits. "What I wanted was to be *in* Menudo. I wanted to give concerts, to travel, to meet the pretty girls."

A Latin pop sensation, Menudo was to young Latin girls what the Beatles had been to Anglos a decade earlier—minus the songwriting talent and musical skills of the latter. Menudo would become the model for later bubble-gum teen groups such as New Kids on the Block and First Edition, which launched the career of R&B bad boy Bobby Brown.

Menudo was the brainchild of pop impresario Edgardo Diaz, who formed the group in 1977. What made his concept unique was that he decided to keep his group perennially young for each new wave of teenage girls by replacing members once they reached seventeen. The concept was to keep the boys at an age that played up to young girls' romanticism and keep the group's sound and image eternally youthful.

"In Spanish, the word *menudo* means 'small' and/or 'change,' " Ricky notes. "So every number of years, the group would change—when you got older you left the group and a young boy joined, because Menudo's appeal to young girls was pubescent sexual tease, not adult sexuality. But the group always had five members."

In the summer of 1978, Menudo became the first Spanish-speaking pop musical group to break the language barrier in the United States, and before you could say *olé*, Menudo was on the cover of every teen magazine.

And as the record sales increased, television and movie producers sought to capitalize on the group's popularity, and in Latin America they appeared on weekly Menudo television specials and even starred in a feature film that broke box office records at the Latin Theater in New York.

After Ricky Melendez, the last of the original members, had left the band, Menudo's management began the search for his replacement. "I read an interview with those guys and they said, 'If you want to join the group you have to come to the management's office, fill out an application form. They'll call you and tell you if they're interested in you or not.' I was hoping they'd take me as his replacement.

"So I filled out an application form and sat and waited for them to call. I took singing and dancing lessons—anything to have more chance of being accepted to that group. Menudo was the first boy-group, by the way."

Ricky was elated when he got a callback and was asked to come in for an audition. But at eleven years old, Ricky was just a little too young to interest the group's management. Ricky was crushed by the rejection, but rather than giving up, having gotten that far made him all the more determined to realize his dream. He auditioned a second time, and again was told he was still too young.

"They searched for the right person for two years," Martin says, "until finally they gave me a third audition and I turned out to be the one they chose."

Literally overnight, Ricky's life changed. And he was

too excited to think about where his new life might take him.

"I was twelve years old and beginning a new life called Menudo," he says. "It was the best overdose of adrenaline. I so badly wanted to be a member of the group, to see the world and to appear onstage, that even my parents were surprised at how easily I was able to leave them."

Ricky, now twelve, was officially the newest member of Menudo. He didn't know it, but his life, and the lives of his family, would never be the same.

2

Getting into Menudo

Life as Ricky had known it was suddenly transformed into a whirlwind of activity. First he had to be blended into the group as its newest and youngest member, which meant he needed a crash course in learning the songs, which came quickly, and the choreography. The other boys accepted him readily, no doubt in part because of his youth and enthusiasm. Because of his rehearsal and work schedule, Ricky had to withdraw from his regular school and instead was tutored by instructors from the Department of Public Instruction of Puerto Rico.

Ricky officially joined Menudo on July 10, 1984, and was quickly enveloped in a life that was comprised of hysterical and adoring young female fans, hit records, draining rehearsal schedules, and bone-wearying touring. He also spent countless hours in the recording studio, where the boys would have to sing an exhausting number of takes until the tracks were just so. Because the Menudo sound depended heavily on harmony, it was critical that Ricky learn to vocalize with precision. He was also schooled in playing to the audience—how to flirt with the young girls who would be mobbing the stage in hopes of just catching one of the boys' eyes or being honored with a smile or a wink. And it was drummed into Ricky that his personal appearance must be clean-cut and well-groomed, as befit the Menudo style.

The expectations on Ricky were high, and he realized almost immediately that as much fun as it was to say he was part of Menudo, and as thrilling as it was to perform in front of screaming fans, Menudo was first and foremost a serious business. Years later he would admit that his time in Menudo wasn't quite what he had expected and that his memories were bittersweet. "Menudo was the best school," he says, adding that if there were two words that best defined the rigors of Menudo, they were *adrenaline* and *discipline.*

"And you can spell those with a capital *A* and a capital *C*. With all the rehearsals and the discipline, it was like the military," he notes. But then he also acknowledges that, "If I think about it and try to put myself in the position of a manager dealing with five kids who are away from home, and consider the responsibility that was on him, I can understand why he had to be tough on us.

"But although he was tough, he was tough with love. So when I say it was like the military, I don't mean we had to stand at attention, salute and stuff like that. But when you're dealing with young kids between the ages of twelve and seventeen, just imagine what boys are like during those years. It doesn't matter if you're in the business or not, you're a mess. You're dealing with a lot of issues. Your hormones are all over the place."

More than anything, it was the touring that opened Ricky's eyes to a world he had only dreamed existed.

While the travel itself was numbing, performing in front of a sea of fans was an adrenaline rush unlike anything he'd ever experienced.

"I joined the group when it was very big in Latin America and so I went straight to the stadiums," Ricky explains. "And it was a little overwhelming, I would say. But one of the good things of being in that band is that I saw two hundred thousand people in one stadium, but I also saw fifteen people in one concert."

Despite Diaz's best effort to keep the boys on a tight leash, no amount of discipline and oversight could prevent his charges from experiencing at least some of the temptations of life on the road. Although on one hand, Menudo presented a clean-cut image, they were also marketed as blatant sex objects, with numerous photo spreads depicting the boys shirtless in seductive poses or in tight bathing suits while lounging on the beach. So it's not surprising that some of the more forward fans happily offered themselves up as groupies. And it's equally unsurprising that Ricky had his first romantic and sexual experiences while on the road with Menudo.

"My first wet kiss was when I was thirteen years old, with the most beautiful girl I have seen up until today," he says, smiling. "But when I was with Menudo, we had many girls. We'd swap girls, too," he admits.

Ricky also experienced a few heartbreaks along the way, too.

"The worst thing that ever happened to me is a girl telling me, 'How much I love you,' then—boom! She broke a bottle on my head. That's it! Love kills sometimes." The year was 1986, and despite the time that has passed, "I still remember her face," he says wistfully.

Although the members of the group were working as adults, every now and then there were distinct reminders that they were still very much children, such as in August 1985, when Ricky and some other members of the group came down with the chicken pox while touring in Orlando, Florida. It was particularly bad timing because the group was preparing to leave on a major tour of Brazil. According to a news report:

> *The group has already canceled dates in Chicago and Providence, Rhode Island, and has been forced to scrap a week of interviews and promotions in Brazil. Afflicted with the itchy blisters are Ricky Martin, 12, Roy Rosello, 15, and Charlie Rivera, 16, who caught the virus from Raymond Acevedo, a newcomer to the group. Acevedo has recovered from the virus.*

What's interesting to note is that there seems to be a discrepancy concerning Ricky's age. If he was born in December 1971, that means he would actually have been 13 and not twelve in August 1985. Either the news report was wrong or they were promoting Ricky to be younger than he actually was. But with the arrival of Ray, Ricky was suddenly no longer Menudo's baby of the family.

Raymond Enrique was born in Puerto Rico on December 21. The son of two teachers, Ray came to the attention of Edgardo Diaz after Ray's dad produced his son singing a Spanish-language version of Donna Summer's "She Works Hard for the Money." Ray joined Menudo in 1985 and first appeared on the *Menudo* album, the group's second English-language album, as lead singer on "You and Me All the Way.'' On the next album, he sang lead on four songs, including ''Me Siento Bien con Mis Amigos,'' on which he shared lead vocals with Ricky.

But regardless of who sang lead vocals, fans flocked to catch a glimpse of their idols. Although Menudo had begun as a Latin American phenomenon, they eventually became popular the world over, from America to Asia.

But no matter what part of the world they traveled to perform, the reaction was universal, such as when they took Singapore and the Philippines by storm in the summer of 1985.

At the time, Menudo was making the girls around the world swoon with their song ''If You're Not Here.'' But ironically, the group had yet to make much of a splash in the Philippines, and when it was announced that they would be performing, some of the unconverted made fun of the group's name, which is also the name of a kind of Spanish food dish. As far as anyone knew, they were simply another rock-and-roll band trying to make some money hopscotching country to country.

But when Menudo touched down in Manila, all that changed. Noted one fan:

> *Imagine, though, the surprise of many when what arrived at the airport were a bunch of good-looking, good-natured, energetic, and wholesome boys. And soon, after guesting in just two TV programs, many teenagers around the country were going gaga over them. Indeed, they have won many Filipino fans with their big ready smiles, waves, and energetic performances. You all have to understand that we Filipinos are generally conservative, and parents*

just won't tolerate having their children idolize people who are rumored to have even bad habits. But with Menudo, parents were much tolerant . . . approving even.

Just as Paul was generally recognized as the favorite Beatle, Robi Rosa, one of Ricky's closest Menudo friends, was usually the object of the most desire by the fans, primarily because he sang lead on "If You're Not Here" and "Because of Love." In fact, if people would have been forced to guess, it would have been Robi voted most likely to succeed post-Menudo. But a close second in the Menudo popularity contest was Ricky, with his sparkling eyes and movie star smile. It also didn't hurt that he was the baby of the group, which appealed to the younger female fans.

By the time Robi, Ricky, and the others left after that first visit, full-fledged *Menudomania* had taken over the Philippines. When they returned to Manila a short time later, their concerts were sold out, and the group remained top teen idols for the next several years running, surprising both the media and music critics.

They particularly endeared themselves to Filipino audiences when Charlie Rivera performed "Nandiyan Ka Na Naman" ("Here You Are Again") in Tagalog, the indigenous national dialect. That gesture won over even the most skeptical observers.

Like the rest of the world, the Philippines simply couldn't resist the quintet of well-scrubbed, shiny-faced young Latin boys. And it seemed wherever they went, concert attendance records fell in their wake. In 1983, Menudo made the *Guinness Book of World Records* for having the largest audiences ever. In March of that year, Menudo performed for 90,000 delirious fans in three sold-out concerts, then one-upped themselves by filling Mexico City's Azteca Stadium to its 105,000-seat capacity. In New York, 88,000 lined up at Madison Square Garden over four nights; a total of 75,000 Filipinos saw Menudo perform during their five-concert stand in that country, and at Cuzcatlan Stadium in San Salvador, El Salvador, 50,000 enthusiastic fans screamed and cheered throughout the boys' concert. The group was so used to huge crowds that playing before the 40,000 people at the National Stadium in Lima, Peru, seemed almost intimate.

In America, the teenagers were profiled in top entertainment and news magazines such as *People, Time,* and *Newsweek*. They also were featured on a variety of television specials and shows, including *Good Morning America, Solid Gold, 20/20, Entertainment Tonight, Now It Can Be Told, Silver Spoons,* The Grammy Awards, the Macy's Thanksgiving Day parade and "Salute to the Statue of Liberty." And if there was any doubt left about their mainstream appeal, it was officially dispelled when they even guest-starred on an episode of that most middle-class of shows, *The Love Boat*.

Menudo merchandising was everywhere, too, including the mandatory lunch boxes, as well as Menudo dolls created in the likeness of the boys. "Yes, I had a doll," Ricky reveals with a laugh. "I still have it. I remember it today like it was yesterday, when they were taking the pictures of me, you know, like in every angle to create the doll. It was great! It was perfectly done, to be honest, my haircut and everything, my eyes, my smile; it was great."

Everywhere they went, masses of humanity followed, and Diaz started using the group's popularity to promote political and social causes. In Colombia, four million people lined the streets to greet Menudo, there to headline the Solidaridad for Colombia event. And in 1984, Menudo was appointed the International Youth Ambassador for UNICEF, acting as a representative for peace. They were also active in antidrug and Stay in School campaigns in various countries.

In Brazil, Menudo became the most popular recording act, besting such high-powered performers as Julio Iglesias and Michael Jackson. Their albums continued to sell into the millions, with *Evolución* passing the four-million mark. Over the course of twenty concerts in their Brazilian tour, Menudo attracted over 1.5 million people, including 200,000 for their Morumbi Stadium appearance in Sao Paulo.

By 1986, the group's staggering popularity had spread far beyond the United States and Latin America to Japan and Italy and every other corner of the world, making them truly international stars. When the group's tenth anniversary world tour was announced in 1987, the American and Latin American concert dates sold out within hours.

But as so often happens, professional success was no guarantee of personal peace and happiness. For Ricky, the rigors and demands of Menudo caused painful conflicts and divisions within his family. Because Ricky spent so much time on the road and so little time in Puerto Rico, his parents, Enrique Martin and Nerieda, began arguing over who Ricky should spend time with when he was home. Although they had legal joint custody of Ricky, their disagreement escalated into a full-blown feud.

"Just as my dreams started coming true, my parents started fighting," Ricky recalls quietly. "I had everything I ever wanted, but my family was falling apart. Before that, I was the glue that kept them friendly toward each other."

Although he was disappointed in both his parents, the conflict took its greatest toll on his relationship with his father. Ricky was particularly angry with his dad because, as a psychologist, he felt his father should have known better than to pit Ricky between two people he loved. "He wanted me to choose between him and my mother. How do you ask a child that?"

Now a teenager, Ricky was so upset over the situation, he changed his name from Enrique and made the decision to live with his mother full-time, creating a rift with his father that would last for almost a decade.

Despite his youth and vigor, the stresses and strain of touring up to nine months a year and rehearsing sometimes as much as sixteen hours a day began to take its toll. Plus, although Menudo was making Ricky famous and making him rich, it was also beginning to frustrate him creatively and, over time, began to affect his desire to perform. Edgardo Diaz called every shot, and Ricky began to resent the manager's autocratic style.

"Our creativity was stifled," Ricky says bluntly. "We were told the songs we wrote were no good." With disenchantment came challenges to Diaz's authority. "We began to question the need for rehearsing the same routines over and over," Ricky admits. "The only thing that bothered me was not being able to express my opinions.

When you entered Menudo, you became part of a well-structured machine that did not need your input.''

Not only was Diaz starting to be scrutinized from within the group, but fans were beginning to criticize his most nonnegotiable rule. Although Menudo became famous in part because of Diaz's insistence on replacing members once they matured, it also became a source of fan backlash. As the time neared for Charlie Rivera, Roy Rosello, and Robi Rosa to be given their send-offs, fans around the world expressed their upset and anger in writing and in teen magazines.

After Charlie left, the Filipino fans in particular were so vocal in their outrage that Edgardo Diaz had Menudo record the song ''I'm Going Back to the Philippines,'' sung by the then-newest member, Ray Acevedo. The song, along with the accompanying video, succeeded in placating fans and introducing Ray. Sergio Gonzales, who replaced Roy Rosello, was the next to join the group, and after a while fans seemed to embrace each new boy. At the same time, though, Diaz knew how important it was to pick the perfect successor for each departing boy, which is why Robi actually stayed on with Menudo six months past his designated forced time of retirement. But one by one, the members aged and left. First Charlie Rivera, then Roy, and eventually Robi would all give their farewell performances in front of often sobbing, hysterical fans.

Although keeping the group eternally young had been the foundation for Menudo's success, replacing the boys would also prove to be the group's ultimate Achilles' heel in some ways. Although graduating members had worked well while the group was still just a Latin American sensation, once Menudo became international stars, fans by the millions became disappointed and disillusioned as they saw their idols, the objects of their romantic desires, forced off the stage and, for the most part, out of the limelight.

And as Ricky watched the other members he'd shared so many experiences with leave, one by one, he became increasingly aware that it was now his turn to start watching the calendar.

3

Leaving Menudo

Considering the immense popularity of Menudo, it was no surprise that several of the individual members hoped to duplicate their success as solo artists. Nor should it really have been much of a surprise at their inability to do so. As part of the collective known as Menudo, their identity was inexorably interwoven with the clean-cut, boy-next-door image of the group. But when finally cut loose from the rigid parameters set by Diaz, the young men immediately sought to express themselves as individuals, but in doing so they became strangers to their fans. Although many of the ex-Menudos retained a core of loyal followers, none were able to project and establish an individual style and image that captured the hearts of fans for any lasting period of time. In other words, they maintained the ex-Menudo label, instead of evolving into individual, stand-alone performers.

It's somewhat ironic that the original Menudo members, who paved the way for much of the later successes, had all left prior to the group's international breakthrough, missing Menudo's glory years, and as a result, none were able to capitalize on their association with the group. Although years later, the original Menudo—Ray, Charlie, Rene, Johnny, Miguel, and Ricky Melendez—reunited to form the group El Reencuentro and enjoyed the benefit of the nostalgia and retro-happy 1990s, as thirty-somethings flocked to relive their childhoods for the group's self-styled reunion tour, which was basically a promotional tool for their album, *El Reencuentro: 15 Años Después.*

Said one critic:

> *On Tuesday, six former members of '80s phenom Menudo got together at Symphony Hall as El Reencuentro. It sounded deadly, but the show actually was a lot of fun. Songs that were annoying when bleated out by high-pitched 13-year-olds were pretty infectious performed by grown men. And a couple of members of the group—Johnny Lozada and Ray Reyes—were so good, it's puzzling why they haven't found more solo success.*

Despite a publicity blitz, which included the members' donation of one of their costumes from their reunion world tour to the Fashion Café in Manhattan, the reformed group only achieved modest success within the Latin community and weren't able to cross over and gain broad appeal.

Of Menudo's second generation, many fans thought that Robi Rosa, whose real name was Robert Edward Rosa Suárez, might be the first to become a huge star as a solo performer. Interestingly, Robi, who was a year and a half older than Ricky, was American by birth, a native of Long Island, New York, but later moved with his family to Puerto Rico, where he had begun his professional career with a group named Admir when Robi was just eight years old.

At first it seemed as if Rosa might live up to the expectations of his supportive fans. After leaving Menudo, Robi spent time in Brazil, where he recorded several albums in Portuguese. In 1988, a year after leaving Menudo, Robi starred in the film *Salsa,* which was panned by moviegoers and critics alike and which earned Robi the dubious honor of being nominated for a Razzie Award as Worst New Star for 1988. Even though the movie failed to help his career, it did change his life. His costar, Angelea Alvarado, later became his wife and the mother to their son, Revel.

When Robi returned to Manila while promoting *Salsa,* fans were shocked at his appearance. Gone was the clean-cut youth of Menudo and in his place was a very adult man, with long hair and visible tattoos covering his arms. But out of loyalty, many of his fans dutifully paid to see the film, which ultimately bombed there as it did everywhere else. Other than a costarring role in the forgettable *Real Men Don't Eat Gummy Bears,* Rosa's film career was over.

With acting not a viable option anymore, in the late 1980s Robi formed his own group, Maggie's Dream. But their debut album failed to generate any heat and the group disbanded, leaving Robi back where he started. Over the years, Rosa, now going by the professional name Robi Draco Rosa, recorded several albums but neither of his subsequent groups, Songbird & Roosters and Sweet & Low, were able to break out of the crowded musical pack. Nor did his solo effort, *Frio*, earn much interest from critics or fans. It wouldn't be until he reteamed with his old friend Ricky Martin that Robi would once again find himself in the limelight.

But the future might as well been another lifetime. To the teenage Ricky, the only moment was the present. After Robi's departure from the band, many longtime Menudo fans concentrated their adoration onto Ricky. However, it eventually became apparent that Menudo might well have hit its peak and was beginning to taper off. Not that the fans disappeared overnight or that record sales plummeted, but there was a perceptible cooling of Menudomania.

Some fans attributed the shift to the emotional toll losing favored members had taken. Says one Filipino fan:

> *The members they loved were gone, and the new members just didn't seem as interesting, or as charming, or as talented as them. So . . . their popularity here died. And while Ricky had grown then and was still adored by many, he had his retirement going against him. After losing four members, with Robby as their biggest loss, Menudo fans just couldn't take it anymore. So they just let Ricky go before he left them. Other new members didn't matter.*
>
> *Robby and Ricky were my favorites, and Menudo were a big part of my adolescence. I practically grew up with them. But I was also affected by the retirement of other Menudo members, and when Robby left, it just broke my heart. So even if Ricky was still in the group, I decided to just let them go.*

Even though the end of Menudo might have been visible on the far horizon, it was still a long way off. Ricky's time with the group was quickly coming to an end, but he couldn't even begin to imagine what life would be like post-Menudo. However, fortunately for Ricky, he had always made a point of not letting the unbelievable attention and popularity go too much to his head.

"Fame can be very disturbing," he admits. "It brings fantasy. I don't need fantasy. I need reality. In fact, people in showbiz should watch out. Fame can hurt. My medicine is my family and friends. Which is why I say I'm nothing without my family. Family for me is very important."

And in the end there would be only his family to go back to when his time with Menudo was over. After five fantastic and often unfathomable years, Ricky's tenure with Menudo came to an end on July 10, 1989.

"Unfortunately, the Menudo rule was that you had to leave the band once you reached seventeen. My last concert was in Puerto Rico, my hometown. I am a man who cries, and I cried a lot," he says of that final performance.

And just like that, he was cut loose and the entire structure of his life seemed to turn upside down. Martin admits he asked himself, " 'What am I doing now?' I was really confused. I'm going to be honest. I thought, 'What's going to happen to me?' "

Now, looking back, Ricky can put his time in Menudo in better perspective and speak dispassionately about what the experience ultimately meant to him and what it meant for him. But one question he doesn't really address is whether he feels that he missed out on too much of his childhood because of the demands of being in the group.

"I don't even want to think about it. Maybe I did, but what's normal, you know? For me, normal was to hop on a plane and do concerts and do press conferences and interviews, and for others maybe what was normal at that time was to go to school and to ride their bike and to have a graduation.

"I had no graduation; my classroom was a hotel room. Of course, I went to school and everything, but those are things I don't want to think about because I'm going to go crazy, and I'm gonna review and say if I was born again I would do it again. I would do it again."

Five years of living out a dream, of performing in front of millions of fans on nearly every continent on the planet, had truly been the experience of a lifetime, but nothing comes without a price; for everything he got, there was something taken away.

"I have no regrets; it was a fascinating journey, a phenomenal experience. My school was the hotel room and the lobby was my playground," he says. "Menudo was a great experience and a great beginning—the best school possible. It taught me to be disciplined. I learned to perform. I learned to be a professional. It was very regimented, like military discipline, which is something that I still practice today. Up to today I like working like that."

Being in Menudo also allowed Ricky a kind of freedom few adolescents get to enjoy. "To be away from home when you're twelve or thirteen gives you a sense of individuality. Yes, I love my parents and I want them to be there forever, but still, they're proud of me because I can make my own decisions."

But for all the benefits of being in the group, hindsight

also convinced Martin that it was time to leave when he did. "I was part of the group for five years, and as great as it was, I felt that it was time to move on. I was exhausted! But the Menudo period was great. If a member of a boy-group reads this, let me give you a tip: use every second that you're part of that group. You learn from everything, and when it's over you can use that knowledge and go and do whatever you want. You have to make people see you as more than just part of that group; I'd hate to still be called Ricky 'ex-Menudo' Martin. But if you go and do new things yourself, that will pass. You just have to prove that you can do more than perform in that group."

Of course, as the others such as Ray learned, that was easier said than done. August 2, 1988, marked Ray Acevedo's last day as a member of Menudo. Curiously, though, there was no farewell concert and no fanfare, just termination. Unlike Robi, Ray seemingly disappeared after leaving the group. He spent time in both Florida and New York for a while and appeared in a few off-Broadway plays. In 1997, he resurfaced when asked to translate a song into Spanish that appeared on an album recording by another ex-Menudo, Ruben Gomez, but then he disappeared into the musical shadows again.

In addition to the fear of being a has-been before reaching legal age, there were other downsides to Menudo. "It was commercialism to the highest degree," Ricky acknowledges, "and I'm not extremely proud about it. But I don't have to apologize, either. It was a great school for me. They would pay us for the records, the concerts, and all the training.

"So I am very grateful, I'm *very* grateful to that band,

because even though I was not allowed to open my mouth because I was part of the concept, still we were loved. We were loved and respected as human beings.''

And they were also paid handsomely for their work. By the time Ricky retired from Menudo, he was a millionaire. Curiously, though, once he left the group, he says he never saw them perform again and lost contact with the other members. However, long after Ricky and Robi and the others with whom he had shared those five years left, Menudo continued on.

In October 1988, in San Antonio, Texas, over two thousand Menudo fans created a small riot when they rushed security guards at a Menudo autograph session and started tearing off the boys' clothes in a frenzy. Police had to be called, and the incident made CNN, *Entertainment Tonight* and all the major TV networks' news.

In April 1990, Menudo released a greatest-hits album, *La Colección,* which sold more than two million copies in Mexico alone. Sales were so brisk that Edgardo Diaz released a second greatest-hits album later in the year, *Menudo La Decada.* And in September 1991, Telemundo, the Spanish television network, announced it would air a weekly *telenova* called *Menudo Mania.*

But times change and musical fashions evolve, and although they still found fans, Menudo was also now considered passé. So in May 1993, Diaz tinkered with his formula and gave Menudo a new sound and a different image, going for more of a street and urban attitude. The then-members recorded English-language songs such as ''Dancing, Moving, Shaking'' and ''Cosmopolitan Girl.'' But no amount of reinvention could change the reality that the glory days were over, and Menudo ultimately disbanded.

For a while. Like the phoenix, Menudo refuses to stay in the ashes, and over the last few years has been resurrected with some changes. Most notably, the group's artistic base has moved from Puerto Rico to Florida, and all the members are English speaking. Regardless of how well the new incarnation does or doesn't do, nothing can take away the group's lasting legacy of having been the greatest musical phenomenon in Latin American history. Their thirty-one albums sold in excess of 20 million copies, and as the song "Dónde Está Tu Amor," proved, they can still top the charts in the later 1990s.

Over the years, there have been over thirty members of Menudo, who recorded songs in five different languages and contributed to the group's overall success. And Ricky felt very honored to be part of that exclusive club. But once it was over, he had to try to figure out what to do with the rest of his life, which seemed to be an endless, lonely road.

Ricky asked himself what he wanted to do. " 'You want to act, you want to sing? Okay.' So I finished high school, then decided, Let's stop for a little while. Let's go to New York. Let's be alone. Let's breathe. Let's connect. Let's do the right choices."

Ricky had left his Puerto Rican home many times as a teenager, but this time when he left, although it would always be his homeland, part of him knew he was leaving for good.

4

A New Career

As Ricky tried to find his post-Menudo place in the world, he was aware that entertainment history was working against him. There had been many teen idols, from Frankie Avalon to David Cassidy, and to one degree or another, all had carried the teen idol label with them well into adulthood. And it was a stigma that many performers found impossible to get past. Also working against maturing teen idols was that in many cases, they neither played instruments nor wrote their own songs, meaning it was the youthful persona they projected that drove their initial careers. Unfortunately, many of those performers weren't nearly as cute as adults as they had been as adolescents.

But even when they maintained striking looks and were musicians in their own right, teen idols have found it difficult to make the transition to a more mature audience.

In a special report on teen idols, *Entertainment Tonight* correspondent Dana Kennedy noted that "Million-dollar contracts, platinum records, all sounds great. But if you make it so big when you're a teenager, can you make your career last? I mean, whatever happened to

Donnie Osmond, New Kids on the Block, Menudo, or the granddaddy of all teen idols, David Cassidy?"

Cassidy, who shot to fame on the 1970s television sitcom *The Partridge Family,* began his career doing dramatic acting roles and playing hard rock on his guitar. But once he became identified as Keith Partridge, nobody wanted to see him as either a dramatic actor or a rock-and-roll musician. He was the King of bubble gum pop with hits like "Come On, Get Happy" and "I Think I Love You."

"I regret not being able to show the dimension that I had and being looked upon almost as a joke. I spent almost ten years completely frustrated. I got as low as you could get. I was licking the curb."

And he notes that not much has changed in expectations toward teen acts. "A lot of people are looking at their watches now, going, 'They've got about another—four, three, two, one—that's about it.' But my own belief is that if you have the talent, you can survive."

But even though Cassidy, who has now forged a career in theater and as a headliner in Las Vegas, managed to survive, Ricky had no desire to wait until his thirties to make the transition. He fully intended to keep pursuing his music as well as acting, even if he didn't know exactly where to begin. His philosophy of simply doing work he was proud of is echoed by current teen phenom Ben Kweller, of the group Radish.

"The way to overcome it," offers Kweller, "is to just keep writing songs, and to keep making records that make us happy, you know, whether or not we are big stars at it, you know, that's what we love to do."

Ricky knew that the key to survival was continued

growth and tackling new challenges and setting new goals for himself—even when others tried to dissuade him.

"I wanted to try something different in show business. A lot of people told me, though, 'If you do acting, you can't do music. And if you do music, you can't do acting.' But I said, 'Why not?' If you take advantage of both, one can feed the other."

After his farewell concert, Ricky decided to take a sabbatical from performing and music. "I did something totally different. I took a break from show business and I disconnected myself from the artistic world. I needed a year off for reflection, catharsis, and maturity.

"It was necessary because my first five years in the business were pure adrenaline, very intense. And because I had to get some rest. But," he adds, "the experience of Menudo turned out to be wonderful, and it gave me more than it took out of me."

So Ricky went back to high school to finish his studies. Although the regular, nonglamorous routine of school seemed alien after so many years of nonstop travel and performing, Ricky didn't feel personally out of place. Despite being an internationally famous performer, Ricky didn't let his fame get in the way of his pre-Menudo friendships.

In between touring and recording, Ricky had continued to hang out with his old friends, in part as a way to keep himself grounded and in part because it was a nice break from the pressure of stardom. With his childhood friends, he could just be himself. Nor did he have to wonder whether they were only his friends because he was in Menudo; these people had liked him when he was just another local kid, and even though he was adored by people the world over, they still treated him like he was one of them.

But after he graduated from high school, Ricky began to experience a restlessness. "I was actually still deciding whether I would continue in show business, because I had had a lot of success already," he admits.

Not only was his future up in the air, but he was still estranged from his father, and the tension between his parents remained thick and uncomfortable. So Ricky made a momentous decision. "I left for New York."

After having missed so much of her son's teenage years because of his commitments to Menudo, Ricky's mother was not happy at his decision to leave home again.

"Oh, no, not at all. Her idea was, 'If you want to take a year off, go to Miami; that's not so far away.' "

But going away was precisely the point. Ricky says he went to New York, and for the longest time, "I did absolutely nothing. That was great! I just sat myself down on a bench and watched the people."

For the first time in his life, Ricky was truly on his own. Although he had spent significant time away from his parents while touring, he had always been under the direct supervision of the Menudo handlers, who were actually stricter than his parents. So in New York, Ricky learned to take care of himself.

"I really needed to be alone, and I did a lot of growing up there," says Ricky, who lived off the substantial savings he had amassed over the previous five years. "In Menudo they told you what silverware to use. Suddenly I was paying my own bills."

Because he didn't need to worry about supporting himself, Ricky was able to concentrate on pursuits that interested him and expanded his creative and personal horizons.

"When I left Menudo, it was my intention to go into acting full-time," Martin admits. "So I took some acting and dancing lessons."

So for a couple of years, Ricky concentrated on studying and waiting for the right opportunities to present themselves. But in the early 1990s, roles for Latin performers were scarce in both American television and film, especially a performer who was still so closely associated with Menudo. For all the group's success, it was still considered a musical gimmick and artistically suspect by many within the entertainment industry.

Although Ricky knew it would take time to reestablish himself as an adult solo performer, he also started to get impatient being away from the stage. About that time, he got a call from a producer who worked in the Mexican television industry.

"He just asked me if I'd like to do some theater work there!" Ricky couldn't believe his luck. He said to the producer, " 'Eh, wait a minute . . . ' then I put my hand on the horn and yelled really hard," so happy he could barely contain his emotions. But knowing the importance of appearing to be professional, he got back on the phone and calmly told the producer, " 'Um, yeah, I could do that, sure. Let me know what you have and I'll think about it.'

"To make a long story short, I left for Mexico."

Mexico City is a place of contrasts. On one hand, it's rich in the country's history, with spectacular museums and artwork. Beautiful plazas and well-tended parks dot the city, with architecture that reflects the heritage of its

Spanish settlers. On the other hand, Mexico City also has its share of crime, and its air is among the most polluted on earth. It's a place where the past and the present collide and struggle for the future, and it would be Martin's home for the next three years.

What the producer had offered Ricky was a chance to immerse himself in both acting and music by starring in the long-running stage musical *Mama Ama el Rock* (*Mom Loves Rock*), which costarred Angélica Vale and Angélica María. Martin was in heaven because "I didn't have to turn my back on music. And being onstage like that fascinated me."

Ricky says he "always wanted to do theater, musical theater. Broadway. London," but was just as happy performing in Mexico.

"Then while I was working in the theater, someone called and asked me to do some television work. It was a soap where I would play a musician, so I could keep on singing as well as acting. Of course I said yes."

It wasn't just any soap Ricky had been asked to join, but the extremely popular daytime drama *Alcanzar una Estrella II* (*Reach for a Star*), in which he played Pablo, the show's resident musician and singer. The producers, well aware of Ricky's former popularity when part of Menudo, hoped that lightning would strike twice. Also, knowing a hot property when they saw one, they wasted no time recruiting Ricky for his musical skills and had him sing the title song of the series.

Life in Mexico City was good to Ricky, and once again he felt vibrant and productive. Years of travel had also made it easy for Ricky to adapt to new environments, and he made friends easily and quickly.

"I had a lot of friends, and I was kind of adopted by this incredible family. They made it so much easier, but I got used to it easily, because I was working a lot."

But Ricky admits that "it was so different just being in another country" for an extended period of time rather than just passing through until moving on to the next tour stop. Most amazing to him was that even though he was in a Spanish-speaking country, the Mexican dialect made it "almost another language."

The only downside to his stay was that he lived in constant fear of being caught in a catastrophic earthquake like the one that leveled much of the city in 1985. In four minutes of geological violence, over 250 buildings in the downtown area collapsed, thousands were made uninhabitable, and several thousand people were killed, with thousands more injured by the magnitude 7.8 tremblor. In a testament to the importance of building codes, one of the few edifices left standing downtown was the American Embassy, which had been built according to U.S. federal earthquake codes.

When he got to Mexico, the memories of the death and destruction were still vivid in the minds of the people there, who would start any time there was even a small tremor. But Ricky managed to conquer his fears by concentrating on his acting work, which he was almost as passionate about as he was his music. "It taught me what it is to be disciplined, something that I still practice today," he says of the rigors of working in the *novela.*

Alcanzar una Estrella II was a hit, making Ricky, along with the rest of the cast, which included a young crop of Mexican stars such as Sasha, Bibi Gaytán, Angélica Rivera, Pedro Fernández, and Erick Rubin, hot properties.

The *novela* was so popular that the producers formed a musical group from the cast, Muñecos de Papél, with Ricky singing the track "Juego de Ajedrez." Naturally, the album was a huge success, which resulted in Ricky and the other participating cast members going on a countrywide tour. It was during that tour that Ricky realized how desperately he missed singing and performing in front of cheering, delirious fans.

"Being back onstage with Muñecos de Papél, which drew crowds of up to sixty-five thousand people for a single concert, I realized that my calling was music and what a beautiful thing it was to sing. That's where it all began."

From that moment on, Ricky says he "devoted myself completely to music. After that, everything that I did in acting had to do with music."

Which wasn't to say Ricky intended to turn his back completely on acting. When *Alcanzar una Estrella II* was spun off into a feature-film version, Ricky reprised his role as Pablo and ended up winning a Heraldo, the Mexican equivalent of an Academy Award, for his performance.

But for as honored as Ricky was with the acting accolades and as much as he thrived on the adoration of his fans, his heart and attention were concentrated on what would be the most important event of his young adult life: recording his first solo album.

5

Going Solo

Ricky knew that he had only one chance to make a first impression as a solo artist. But if he was going to break out, Mexico was as good a place to try as any. During his Menudo days, the Mexican fans, along with the Brazilians, had been among the most fanatical. That history, plus his newfound success with *Alcanzar una Estrella II,* the album of the same title having sold over a million copies, convinced Ricky there was no time like the present to see if he would connect with audiences on his own. Although he was familiar as an ensemble member, first with Menudo, then with Muñecos de Papél, the biggest question was, could he captivate an audience standing by himself onstage? Did he have the presence and charisma to carry a concert—and an album—entirely on his own?

These were the unanswered questions record labels needed to ponder in deciding whether to sign Ricky as a solo artist. Ultimately, the unknowns regarding Ricky were decidedly outweighed by what *was* known: He was a young man who was associated with selling millions of albums throughout Latin America; he was a popular television and film actor in his own right; he had a solid, mellifluous singing voice; and he had matured into a well-built, 6'1'' young man with matinee-idol good looks. Although Ricky had let his hair grow to his shoulders, his wavy locks served only to accentuate his boyish charms.

In light of the whole package Ricky offered, though, it was an easy decision for Sony Music Mexico executives—they had little to lose and a major star to gain by signing Ricky for his first solo album. So for the first time in his life, he showed up at the recording studio alone, which filled him with both excitement and nerves. This was his moment, and the direction of his future depended largely on whether he was ready for it.

Ricky's debut album, the self-titled *Ricky Martin*, was released in 1991, and within a few weeks the record label knew they had a winner on their hands. Of the ten songs included on the album, five—''Fuego contra Fuego,'' ''Dime que Me Quieres,'' ''Susana,'' ''El Amor de Mi Vida,'' ''Ser Feliz,'' and ''Vuelo''—eventually became top-ten hits, and the album quickly went gold, meaning it sold more than 500,000 copies around the world, in countries including Puerto Rico, Mexico, Colombia, Chile, Argentina, and the United States, making *Ricky Martin* one of Sony's most successful Latin debut albums ever.

But for Ricky, the most special moment came when he first heard himself on the radio as a soloist.

''Well, I have to be really honest. The first time I heard my song on the radio I cried. Men do cry. It's a very healthy habit.'' Although he had heard himself in Menudo songs on the radio before, the experience was entirely different when it was his lone voice singing.

"Well, I mean as a band it still counts, but as a soloist I started crying, I was so happy. I was in Mexico City and it was early in the morning. I knew that my music was about to start getting airplay, so I said, 'Okay, this is it. What do we have to start doing now?' " he says of sitting by the radio, waiting anxiously, listening and wondering, " 'What's coming up next?' "

Hearing himself on the radio filled Ricky with a rush of emotions. "The first thing that came into my head was longevity," he recalls. "I didn't want this to just be something for the summer, and up till today I still think that way. I like to live one day at a time because yesterday doesn't exist anymore and tomorrow doesn't exist yet, so today let's take advantage of what's happening today."

Even today, after all his success, Ricky still follows that philosophy. "If you worry about yesterday and tomorrow too much you don't live today, and it sucks because you have no personality eventually. I want to sit with you in ten years and talk about music and life, so when I go into a studio I think about it that way and it could be a motto for me. Well, one of them anyway. I have a thousand mottoes and missions that I have to accomplish," Ricky admits.

"One is to break stereotypes, when it comes to Latin sounds and images and colors; one of them is to have longevity as a performer and not be just a flash; and another is to constantly grow as an entertainer. That's why I did a bit of theater and acting and, of course, music. And, of course, to be surrounded by the right group of people who are very creative."

As any solo artist knows, it's extremely important to tour, especially when promoting a first album. Ricky scheduled an ambitious slate of performances, and for the first time, he was also the lone performer onstage.

"All the responsibility is now on my shoulders," he noted at the time, then laughed. "I had shared the stage with five guys, and it was amazing. But now I don't want to share the stage with anyone. And after being onstage alone, you don't want to share it with anybody again!"

Nor did he need to. Having been in a teen-idol group had taught him the discipline and the presence needed to command the attention and affection of an audience. And unlike the meticulous and regimented choreography of Menudo, Ricky's solo show was more spontaneous, which added a level of unpredictability and excitement.

"Yes," he says with a laugh. "I'm very happy that I'm alone onstage. Nothing is choreographed. We let the energy flow, and whatever comes out, comes out."

For Ricky, performing is "very addictive, and I would say I cannot live without it. There's nothing like being onstage and just sharing feelings with the audience with only the help of your musicians and your microphone. 'Come on, let's dance together.' It's *fantastic!* It's *fascinating*, to hear people singing your music; to see them dancing and just their reactions.

"For two hours, you're so vulnerable. They touch you and you cry. They touch you and you get angry. They touch you and you'll be happy again. Music says it all. And with all the passion in the songs, you have to leave your skin onstage."

Ricky's first tour, confined to Latin America, was a testament to endurance. He performed 120 concerts, and suddenly it was Rickymania. Everywhere he went he was greeted by screaming fans, all calling his name alone. Along the way he broke several attendance records and won a variety of awards, including the Lo Nuestro award, and many Eres awards. In Venezuela, he won a Silver Orchid for being the most popular performer.

In addition to letting his music speak for itself, Ricky was also skilled at extending himself to his audience, such as when he would sing in Portuguese when appearing in Brazil. Between his stage presence, the attention he paid to his audience, and the infectious melodies of his songs, both the tour and the album were monster successes, and his record label, Sony, rushed Ricky back to Mexico and into their recording studio to work on his sophomore release.

Me Amarás (You'll Love Me) was released in 1993 and was an even greater hit, with its mix of heavily romantic and catchy tunes. But audiences who flocked to see Ricky on this tour noticed that he was maturing not only as a performer, but as a young man. The wild, wavy hair was replaced by a slightly more sophisticated look, and Ricky himself seemed more toned, more hunky. And the girls went crazier than ever before.

But not only did Ricky appeal to young girls, but he also had a solid core of male fans, because he seemed like the regular kind of guy who could be a buddy. And his manner toward the women in the audience was less seductive than playful and respectful. He didn't present himself as a ladies' man, so both men and women could see him as a friend.

When he was in Menudo, Ricky had enjoyed the devotion of fans, so that in itself was nothing new. What was different being a solo act was that there was nobody else onstage to dilute the white-hot glare of the fans. Night after night, it was Ricky alone who basked in the fantasies, desires, and love of the audience.

In February 1993, he performed at the Viùa del Mar music festival in Chile, where he won the crowd over so thoroughly that the audiences brought him back for three encores. It was obvious to all there that Ricky had blown away the other performers, and he was presented with the festival's Silver Seagull award, making him king of the festival.

If all the fan adulation wasn't enough to turn his head, he was also surrounded by record company people who never missed an opportunity to say how great he was, how special. It's a compliment to his upbringing that Ricky was able to keep his ego in check and not be taken with himself, to stay grounded and down-to-earth.

Ricky says he kept from believing his own press releases by remembering a few important lessons. "First of all, being grateful for whatever people are saying. Being grateful to critics both good and bad. Also by staying friendly, being willing to say, 'Hi. Nice to meet you; my name is Ricky.' "

Ricky also kept his priorities in order by not playing it safe. Had he wanted, he could have never ventured out of Latin America and would have been a very successful performer. But Ricky wanted to test himself and push himself, and performed in countries where he wasn't so well known.

"Latin America is basically a lot of countries united by one language, but they are all different cultures. And I could be happy in Latin America with pockets full of money,'' Ricky said once in an interview. ''But for me, to go to Europe and say, 'Hey, nice to meet you; my name is Ricky Martin and this is what I have when it comes to music,' and to talk about yourself without any one knowing you is so healthy for me, after being who I am in Latin America, to be honest.''

It was a formula he would repeat later in Asia, Australia, and eventually America. But there was another, more introspective side of Ricky, too.

''Something else that helps me stay grounded is seeing myself from outside and looking in. To step out of it and look in. Then make the right decisions and step back in saying, 'All right.' And,'' he adds emphatically, ''not to hurt others.''

Keeping in touch with his family, whether by phone, personal contact, or just emotionally, was also vitally important to Ricky, particularly while touring. While some performers carry good-luck charms of some sort with them on their travels, Ricky's talismans were personal in nature.

''I am not superstitious, so I don't have a mascot that I take with me. But I always take photos: of my grandmother, the most beautiful person on earth, and of my mother. They're very important to me, and they give me support and strength when I need it.''

The singles from the second album rocketed Ricky to the top of the Latin music charts and earned him *Billboard*'s New Latin Artist award at the 1993 music awards. But after his *Me Amarás* tour, Ricky abruptly pulled back. As he had done for those eight months in New York, he slowed down in order to gain some perspective on where he was as a singer and as a person. It was also, in part, a strategic business decision.

"I decided to take another break so people wouldn't lose interest in me too fast."

With *Me Amarás* eventually going triple platinum in worldwide sales, the likelihood of fans forgetting about Ricky were slim, but Ricky knew that as his career blossomed, he needed to approach it in a professional, well-thought-out manner. From the moment he sat alone listening to his first released song on the radio, Ricky had worked almost nonstop.

"At first I worked for the fun of it, but now it has become a must because I want to stay at the top," he admitted. "I know I want to do this for the rest of my life. I'm sure I can go even further. I'm surrounded by great people who are very creative, and I'm hungry for more success."

Ricky took careful stock of his career and where he wanted to go with it. While his primary passion remained singing, Ricky still wanted to act as well. Also, he knew that until he conquered American audiences, he would feel as if he had not completely arrived as a performer. Although he had enjoyed amazing success while living in Mexico and had seen his career explode in a short period of time, Ricky believed it was time to move on and to embrace new challenges.

It wasn't that he was tired of Mexico. "Oh, no, I will go back there anytime." It was just that he felt he had accomplished as much as he could by staying there. "So I went to Los Angeles," Ricky says, in hopes of making his presence known in the United States either through his music or his acting.

So in the late summer of 1993, Ricky packed his bags and hopped a plane for Los Angeles, put his destiny in the hands of fate, and counted on his considerable talents to lead the way. However, the road to true superstardom would take some unexpected twists along the way.

6

Checking into *General Hospital*

It is inevitable that even the most charmed lives and careers will suffer a setback or two, and Ricky was no exception to this rule of fate. In 1993 he had an unusual one-two punch of misfortune, which he now calls "a very strange bad streak."

The first incident happened when he was touring in Buenos Aires and he was involved in an automobile accident, when the car he was driving flipped off the road. Although he was not seriously injured, it did bang him up and scared him at how much worse it might have been.

The second incident was far more serious. Ricky was due in San Diego for an interview and flew there in a small plane. The plane took back off after depositing Ricky safely, but a short time later ran out of fuel and crashed, killing the pilot. Almost immediately news spread that it was Ricky who had died in the crash, and fans the world over were hysterical.

"I wasn't there but it was very tough for me," Martin says, who grieved for the dead pilot. He also realized that it very well could have been him on that plane.

"Apparently, though," he said thoughtfully, "I still have a reason to be around."

For the third time in as many years, Ricky had come to live in a new city. Where Manhattan had been a place for him to hide out, and Mexico City a place where he found himself as an adult performer, Los Angeles would be where Ricky would lay the foundation for the rest of his career. It would also serve as a gauge as to how far he yet had to go.

In the early 1990s, Latins were becoming more vocal about television's failure to represent them in any kind of consistently positive way on the small screen, so in a way it was good timing for Ricky, as broadcasters felt pressure to at least make a show of trying to increase the Latin presence on TV.

Although Ricky wasn't deluged with the kinds of offers he would have had had he stayed in Mexico, he was called out for auditions, and in a relatively short period of time landed his first work in American television, appearing in two episodes of the short-lived series *Getting By,* as the character of Martin. The sitcom had been developed as a comeback vehicle for former *Laverne and Shirley* star Cindy Williams, playing a single mom who moves in with a divorced mom, played by Telma Hopkins.

The series debuted in March 1993 on ABC but was canceled two months later. In an unusual turn of events, NBC then picked the show up and put it in their fall lineup. However, the show fared no better on its new network and was canceled at the end of the 1993–94 season.

Even though the show failed to live up to expectations, it was a wonderful springboard for Ricky. His guest appearance on *Getting By* caught the eye of the producers of *General Hospital,* ABC's longest-running and most popular soap, who contacted Ricky's agent and arranged a meeting. It was a case of being in the right place at the right time and having the right ancestry.

"I really wanted to do something on American TV, and they were looking for a Spanish-speaking guy who could sing and act," recounts Ricky.

"Our head writer saw the tapes of Ricky in concert," recalls producer Wendy Riche, "and said, 'Wow! If he can act, let's sign him up.' "

Ricky could, so they did. "They found me, I did an audition, and that was it."

Well, there was actually a little more to it than that. In fact, Ricky's manager, Ricardo Cordero, a fellow Puerto Rican native, was following a carefully thought-out plan he had devised in 1990 to bring Ricky to mainstream America.

"We knew he could sing, dance, and act like few others," explains Cordero. "But we wanted to make sure everyone knew that this was not an aspiring actor, but a well-established star in Latin America."

To secure Ricky a role on *General Hospital,* Cordero sent videos and copies of his client's albums to network producers at ABC. Then he invited them to come see Ricky live at selected concerts in South America that also happened to be sellouts. Not only did Ricky get the part of Miguel, but he was also signed to do a movie of the week and a series pilot. Films would come later.

"Of course, we'd like Ricky to make movies," said his manager, "but the main thing is not to rush him. You know, in Mexico, if you are cute, you have work. But in America, you have to act.''

Being cast in the soap was not just important for Ricky, but for all Latin actors. He represented the new trend of Hispanic actors being accepted more into mainstream television, particularly on soaps. Around the time Martin was recruited for *General Hospital,* Ecuador-born Diego Serrano joined the cast of *Another World.*

''The thing I love most about the show is that I play a very positive character,'' said Serrano, who was concerned about being a positive role model. ''I play a high school senior who likes trigonometry and to study.

''When I auditioned for the role, I was so glad to see that they were doing Tomás as a positive character,'' Diego continued. ''I think it's about time society accepts us for what we are. Too many times they typecast us in negative roles. This is a way we can let Americans know that not all Latin guys are in gangs or are killers.''

Lilly Melgar, who played Ricky's *General Hospital* love interest, Lily, was pleased at being offered a role in the venerable daytime drama.

''I always wanted to be an actress,'' Melgar, whose parents came to America from El Salvador, said in an interview from that time. ''It was like this hidden dream I had. As a child I would always tell people that I wanted to be a Charlie's Angel. So, of course, my ultimate goal is to be a film actress. And this is great experience and preparation for that.

''I was a big fan of *General Hospital* all through my teenage years. So being on this show is a dream come true for me. You see, I didn't want to be on just any soap. I wanted to be on *General Hospital,* and here I am!''

Of course, not everybody was as optimistic as Melgar. Although Rita Gomez, a longtime character actress who played Maria, a housekeeper, on *The Bold and the Beautiful,* for four years, believed that Ricky, Serrano, Melgar, and others could open the door for other Hispanics, to her the doors still seemed as tightly closed as ever.

"I wish I could say it's changed since the forties and fifties when I first came to Los Angeles, but it hasn't," said Gomez.

However, she acknowledged that young performers like Ricky are the only hope. "My advice to young actors and actresses is to stay away from the housekeeping and maid roles. They'll typecast you, and then you'll stay there for the rest of your life."

But being young and relatively untouched by Hollywood casting bias made actors like Ricky and Lilly have a much brighter outlook than older actors like Gomez.

"I believe that we belong to a different generation of actors who are going to change things for the better," Melgar states. "Look at me. I'm not playing a Hispanic maid with an accent on *General Hospital.* I'm playing a rich Catholic girl. So I think we're pioneers in this industry. And I'm proud and happy to be a part of the changes that are coming."

Lilly says she gets her positive thinking from her mother, Lillian, a successful businesswoman. "I'm lucky to be her daughter. We're very similar. We've both been blessed with charisma and a positive attitude. By believing in me she helped me believe in myself. She told me nothing was impossible; anything can come true."

Although Lilly was encouraged by her mother in her dreams to be an actress, her father urged his daughter to go to college, which she did for a while. But the desire to perform was too strong, and after being crowned Miss Salvador L.A., Lilly began her acting career. She was thirty-two when she was hired to play twenty-three-year-old Ricky's on-screen love interest.

Ricky made his first appearance as Miguel Morez on February 17, 1994. His character had come to the soap's fictional city of Port Charles to study natural science and to support himself, and found work as a part-time orderly at General Hospital. As his story line developed, it became clear there was more to Miguel than met the eye.

"Miguel has a lot of secrets, and one of them is that he used to be a singer in Puerto Rico," explained Ricky.

In a real casting coup, the producers wrote an episode where Miguel travels to New York and, while visiting a recording studio, meets up with Julio Iglesias, who encourages Miguel "to go back to my singing career in spite of the past."

Of course, the producers made sure to work in plot lines that allowed Ricky the chance to perform on the show. And in keeping with their efforts to make him a bona fide soap hunk, Martin crooned love ballads.

Even so, Miguel wasn't intended to have quite the vocal prowess that Ricky possessed, so at times Morez's singing leaves a bit to be desired, such as in one episode where he sings "Happy Birthday to You" completely off-key. Ricky just hoped that the audience realized "it was *supposed* to be off-key."

Other than his ability to sing off-key, Ricky liked his small-screen alter ego. "He's passionate towards everything—music, school, friends—and he hates injustice," Ricky said of Miguel, who was written as a fully fleshed-out character and not as a stereotype. Playing a genuine person helped Ricky immediately connect with the audience.

"The mail response on him was very positive," said Wendy Riche, executive producer of *General Hospital.* "Ricky will be very big."

And as they'd hoped, female fans responded to Martin with lusty acceptance. But despite being thrust into the role of daytime sex symbol, or maybe because of it, Ricky was evasive about his personal life, claiming, "I went through that already. Now I have other priorities, and they are to live one day at a time. I'm not dating, but I am growing up."

Of course, his on-screen romantic entanglements were enough. Eventually the mystery surrounding Miguel's past, and the part Lily played in it, was revealed to be yet another tragic soap case of star-crossed lovers. Miguel and Lily had been lovers back in their native Puerto Rico, but once Lily's father found out, he forbade his daughter to see Miguel again. Later she discovered she was pregnant with Miguel's love child, which her father forced her to give up for adoption. Once they were reunited in Port Charles, Lily and Miguel set out to find their long-lost son, Juan.

Aside from the typically farfetched story line, Ricky's experience on *General Hospital* was a decidedly positive one.

"For me, *General Hospital* has been an incredible way of learning and growing as an actor. I look at it as a training school that's going to help my acting career," said Martin at the time. "I think this will even help me in my musical career. At concerts, I'm always in front of the public, and acting gives you more self-confidence.

"During the time I was doing *General Hospital,* I was working on myself as a person. When you work on a soap opera, you work against the clock. For example, if you do a film, you can spend three days on one scene. But in television you only have forty-five minutes. So you have to get your juices flowing; you have to be in touch with yourself."

And one of the things Ricky learned about himself was that his continued estrangement from his father was leaving him with an emptiness inside his heart and soul that he longed to fill. He realized that life was too short to be consumed by anger and resentment over something that happened so many years ago.

After contacting his father and working through what had happened, Ricky was able to come to terms with his dad.

"I hated the estrangement and couldn't live with it anymore," says Ricky. "Now he and I talk almost every day."

The reconciliation was like a weight lifting off of Ricky's strong shoulders, and it brightened his spirits so much, his costars couldn't help but notice.

"After he reconciled with his father, Ricky's been the happiest I've ever seen him," said Melgar. "He has inner peace."

Ricky also had the world at his feet. In addition to ABC approaching Martin about possibly developing a prime-time series with him, Ricky was working on his next album. But while others might have been amazed at how rapidly his career seemed to be flourishing, to Ricky, it was simply the result of believing in himself.

"I guess the things that have worked for me are to be stubborn, *to be stubborn.* If you want something, as long as it doesn't hurt others, go for it. And you know what—have it in your mind. It's like Deepak Chopra says: when you want something it will be yours. If you put it in your mind the whole cosmos will do something for you to get it. Maybe it's not tomorrow, maybe it's not the day after tomorrow, maybe it's in five years, but eventually it *will* be yours.

"But at the same time, start getting ready for whenever you have it in your hands—you can manage it, you can control it, so when it comes to music, be surrounded by great people, creative people, people that are honest, and be yourself."

Ricky also believed in surrounding himself with people who loved him, such as his parents. "They're very proud, but they're there telling me good and bad, good things and bad things if it's necessary, they're there to pull my ears, and I need it.

"We have a great relationship, and we have great communications. They are both parents to me and my friends, and that's not an easy thing to accomplish. But I can talk to my mother as well as to my father, and they're very objective. It's great."

So was his life at the moment. He was appearing in *General Hospital,* his albums continued to sell around the world, he was still in demand as a performer, he now lived in a stylish home in the tony Hollywood Hills area, and his relationship with his family was stronger than ever. If Ricky had a problem, it was that there were not enough hours in the day. Between *General Hospital* and his next album, Ricky was living on overdrive—but he was loving every minute of the ride.

7

Climbing the Charts

Ricky's third album would be a musical bellwether for him in several ways. For the first time in his solo career, he began to concentrate on writing songs, too, rather than just picking songs written by others. It was a challenge but one Ricky relished, drawing inspiration from a variety of sources, some unexpected.

"My influences in music are everywhere. I love Paul Simon, Julio Iglesias, Ruben Blades, and I think Aerosmith is awesome," Martin says of his eclectic musical tastes. But while he appreciated all styles of music and the talents of many singers and songwriters, there was one in particular he found to be a source of inspiration.

"Julio Iglesias is my godfather in music," Ricky says reverentially. "I have been able to work with him and he's given me many words of wisdom. I really do admire him. But," Martin adds emphatically, "I don't want to be him. But I want to follow in his steps, if you know what I mean. He is a very wise man."

Ricky also laughs off the oft-repeated rumors that he is really the illegitimate love child of the famous Latin crooner. "Where do people read this stuff? Julio is someone that I respect a lot. I thought *I* was a workaholic, but Mr. Iglesias is amazing. And with women he is number one."

With writing, Ricky was able to feel even more involved in the overall tone and direction of the album and enjoyed looking for musical hooks and emotions for lyrics in the world around him.

"Inspiration can come anywhere, anytime. It can come sitting in front of the ocean and walking around the city, seeing different faces. I try to look into someone's eyes and see what they're thinking. At the same time, you can be driving and right in the middle of a traffic jam, you read a bumper sticker and—*boom!*—it's there. The one thing you learn, though," he says with a laugh, "is that you need a pen and paper with you all the time!

"But I definitely I think I have a lot of things that I can share. And I've already begun working on material for my *next* album."

The third album also reunited Ricky with an old friend from his musical past, Robi Draco Rosa. "Yes," Ricky excitedly told fans, "Robi is the coproducer of the album, and he's doing really good in his solo career." Working with his former Menudo singing mate, according to Martin, was "great!" Rosa also helped write some of the songs on the album as well.

After months of doing double duty, rushing from the set of *General Hospital* to the recording studio and back, Ricky's third album, *A Medio Vivir* (*To Live by Halves*) was released June 22, 1995, and instinctively he knew it was his best album to date. Not content simply to have another album of strictly Latin sounds, Ricky crafted *A Medio Vivir* to reflect his pop and rock-and-roll influences.

Ironically, although it cemented his musical superstar status in Latin America, Europe, and Australia, it did little for his musical career in America, although whenever he performed, such as at a previous concert at the Universal Amphitheater in Los Angeles, the audience could not stop dancing, nor screaming out Ricky's name. Plus, American women of all ages were beginning to understand the appeal Ricky already had elsewhere in the world. Yes, he was a good actor, of course he was a talented singer, without question he was a gifted presence and performer onstage, but he was also cute and sexy.

Suddenly Ricky found himself deluged with questions on all things romantic, beginning with his personal life. At one point after joining the soap, Ricky said he had a girlfriend, the host of a Mexican television show whom he had met when he was eighteen, but whom he would not name. "She's not an actress; she's not a singer. You never know what will happen, but we're happy the way we are."

But later he announced that they had broken up and that he was "single, very single, at the moment." And he swore he wasn't just saying that to make his female fans feel better.

"No. If I was in love, I would scream it as loud as I could. Love is wonderful; you should share it. I have no problem with talking about love. But if people ask me a million times questions like, 'Who is your ideal woman?' or 'Do you have a girlfriend?' they're going to reach a dead end very soon. So if people ask me a stupid question about love, I start talking about music."

That said, Ricky will talk about what he finds appealing in a woman. "Yes, I like the women who have the beautiful skin and big eyes. And I find legs erotic, but what really arrests me is her smell. And if I never see her again I go mad.

"I like the Latin women, because they have my idiom and my blood. But I would marry a German woman—if she could cook Latin foods."

Food, as it turns out, is of primary importance to Ricky. "Boom! It takes me back home. I love cooking. I will never die of hunger. I'm like, *Bam, bam, bam.* 'Let's do it. Can you bring me that? Can you bring me that, too?' That's cooking. That's the way I cook. I love cooking."

Because he was becoming known for his love ballads, Ricky was frequently asked his philosophies of love, which are best described as bittersweet.

"When you're in love, even though it's wonderful, you also suffer. Love makes you cry. Always. Because of the passion. Especially with impossible love. The impossible love is sometimes one we have to accept."

In any event, Ricky doubted that, at the current stage of his life, it would be possible to have a steady relationship. "No, I think that to travel constantly makes it too complicated, because a woman looks for a more stable life. It's difficult, because at the moment my priority is my career.

"Years ago, I would have given up everything and would have done anything for love—but not now. Maybe that's because I haven't met the right woman. But I do think I will someday get married. And I will have many children. My dream always has been to have a family."

Ricky admits that he often thinks about his own loves

and losses when he sings. "I don't know about others, but I like to speak of things that I have lived. Everything which appears in the lyrics of my songs I have lived one way or another."

And as far as what can make love last, Ricky has no doubt. "Within the love, it is necessary that friendship exists," he says. "That's why it is always necessary to take care of the friendship. For me, the friendship is fundamental, and as far as the love, there are many people who confuse passion with love."

Whether you call it love, passion, or lust, women felt it in abundance for Ricky, who took the label of heartthrob with good-natured reserve.

"It's fun if you want to have fun with it, but it scares me at times. My priority is to do good music, not to look good. Sexuality and sensuality are things that I keep for my own room.

"Sorry, but I don't know what being a sex symbol means. That's an image that's created by the media. They made that up and imposed it on me from the beginning. On the contrary, I'm a very spiritual guy. I'm not what my exterior image, my appearance, reflects, but what develops on the inside, in my heart and my soul."

When asked about the enduring stereotype of the Latin lover, perpetuated by American films, Ricky was thoughtful.

"I'm Latin and I'm also a lover, but I don't know. It's funny because, to some people, being Latin *means* passion—blood, heat, tragedy. And yet that's all very Shakespearean and Shakespeare wasn't Latin. He wrote *Romeo and Juliet,* which is about killing yourself to be with your love—but he was an Englishman."

Not that it was necessarily a bad stereotype, as they go. "When it comes to being Latin, it's not as bad as saying that we are the equivalent of *West Side Story*—with the gangs and mafia, the cocaine and stuff. So given a choice, I guess it's better to be known as a lover than a fighter. I'm very proud of my culture, and I understand that stereotypes come from ignorance. The best way to change minds is to teach people."

But from what his fans saw, Ricky was the ultimate Latin lover—sexy, fun, and likable. Once a fan asked Ricky if he had ever serenaded a girl with his own songs.

"You know, in Puerto Rico it's illegal. Because we're so loud, people would complain if a girl was being serenaded at three A.M. But I lived in Mexico City for five and a half years and it's legal there, so sometimes I would go to a plaza full of mariachi bands and we would get a bunch of us together and go to a friend's house to dance, sing, and play. It wasn't actually a serenade, but it could get romantic."

Since he had joined the soap, the number of Ricky's performances had dwindled, and with the release of his third album he was itching to get back onstage, which he missed tremendously.

"I've been performing onstage since I was six years old—and I still haven't found a word that can describe these feelings. To name a few: power, self-assurance, adrenaline, strength. . . . It's addictive and it's fascinating. One hour onstage makes up for years of hard work. Being onstage is addictive," Martin admits. "You know, you need that immediate reaction. I mean, I'm used to that and I need it and I look for it. I look forward to seeing people's faces.

"Acting is great, and, in fact, improving my acting techniques helped me a lot when I went back in the studio to interpret songs better, because it helped me get in touch with my feelings in a faster way.

"But," Ricky added, "if you asked me if I would do it again, today I would say no, because my priority is music. I'm enjoying every minute of it. This is my baby, I have to take good care of it, once again because I'm dealing with longevity. This is very important for me now."

As usual in a Ricky Martin album, *A Medio Vivir* contains both upbeat dancing music and romantic ballads, which Ricky felt were his forte.

"I usually sing romantic songs. Where I come from is printed in that music, it's printed on that paper that becomes music later on. I'm romantic. It's in me. Hey, I believe a flower says more than a thousand words."

The song destined to become arguably his most famous to date, "Maria," deals with romance, but in a bouncy sort of way. It was also one of Ricky's personal favorites, having been written by Ian Blake, K. C. Porter, and L. Gomez Escolar.

This was a song that Ricky had fashioned from real life. " 'Maria' describes, a little bit, a friend of mine. She's a girl who plays with your head. She first says yes and then says no, and that can drive you crazy. She's no one in particular, but I've been out with girls like Maria."

Even though Ricky claimed that "Maria" wasn't about any one person, he admitted that he had known girls who inspired songs. "Not just songs, but whole albums. Unfortunately, it's usually after you break up with someone and the pain is still raw that you find the need to express it in a very dramatic way. That's when it becomes music.''

But in the case of ''Maria,'' Martin finally reveals that the real genesis of the song was an effort to use a computer to help with music composition.

'' 'Maria' was actually a very intense computer program. I wanted to get closer to my roots, to my culture. We started digging around, looking for sounds and rhythms on the computer, and that's how it came about—it wasn't any specific girl. I mean, Maria *could* be anyone—even someone's dog. It's not about someone special. I can be very romantic—stupidly romantic, actually—but not in this case.

''When you talk about lyrics, 'Maria' is very danceable, rhythmically. It's very rich rhythmically. And it's very romantic. Listen to it.''

People all around the world did listen. And he was winning converts in the United States as well, who found it impossible to sit still while listening to the infectious ''Maria'' and Ricky's other songs. Performing with his nine-piece band and two dancers, Ricky performed to a sellout house at New York's famed Radio City Music Hall in March of 1996 and to a standing-room-only crowd in Miami.

Just by the crowd response, Ricky knew that, little by little, he was making progress in conquering his newly adopted country. And when he let himself think about how much success he had already enjoyed in the previous few years, all he could do was thank the heavens and continue making career choices based on instinct and business savvy.

''I think my success has little to do with destiny. This

industry is a chess game and you have to know how to move the pieces to go forward. I want to do this forever, and it's not destiny but making the right choices that will give my career a future.

"Of course, I know that my career will eventually reach a point where I pull back and this will become a part-time job. What I thought was that I'd spend six months of each year onstage, and the rest of the year I'd spend resting, writing, maybe even directing, because that's something I'd love to do. But," he added, "in the meantime, I'll just keep working."

Little did Ricky know, his workload had only just begun.

8

Debuting on Broadway

In January 1996, Ricky left *General Hospital* to embark on a 150-city concert tour to promote *A Medio Vivir.* His character, Miguel, was written out of the show by having the character also go on an extended road tour. Since the character wasn't killed off, Ricky noted that he "could always come back." But fate would have a different plan for Ricky.

In the spring of 1996, Ricky and his band did a concert in Miami, a city Ricky instantly fell in love with. The tropical beaches, Latin influences, distinct musical sounds, constant action, and nightlife reminded him of Puerto Rico. And he knew in his heart that as soon as he could, he would make Miami his American base—whenever that might be.

While in Miami, as he always did when performing in a city, Martin devoted significant time to interviews and other publicity and promotional activities. It was there, during an interview, that Ricky recalls "a journalist asked me, 'What do you still have to do to be able to die a happy man?'

"When I left the band at first for a period of maybe a year or a year and a half I did nothing. I was just getting to know myself after all that rush; the first thing I did was theater. I went back to the spotlight, you could say, with a musical play I did in Mexico City. Then I did TV, then I did a soap opera, then I did film, and then I went to music again later. It was okay but there was something missing, something I hadn't done.

"So I said, 'I just have to play Broadway once. I want to act in a theater in New York.' And believe it or not, one of those Broadway producers read that article! So he called me and simply offered me a role in *Les Misérables!*" Ricky recalls, still amazed.

Just as he had when the Mexican producer had offered him *Mama Ama el Rock* in Mexico City, Ricky admits, "I was yelling again, 'Of course . . . Um, well, send me some material and I'll see if I can fit it into my schedule.' "

The man who happened to read the interview and called, Richard Jay Alexander, was the executive producer of *Les Misérables*. And in truth, Ricky told him, "I said it doesn't matter what I do, I'll do it."

Ricky saw himself as someone that nontheatergoers might actually pay to go see. "I'm for people who probably otherwise wouldn't go to the theater. So that's what I did."

The role offered to Ricky wasn't the lead character, Jean Valjean, which at the time was played by Craig Schulman, but Marius, who just so happens to be the young male romantic figure of the musical, who falls in love with Valjean's beautiful daughter, Cosette.

"Yes, the only woman in my life is Cosette," he joked

at the time. But he teased his fans by reminding them, "You never know when Cupid comes with his arrow."

To prepare for his role, in addition to rehearsing his lines and learning the blocking, Ricky sat through seventeen performances, watching the man he'd be temporarily replacing, Tom Donoghue. (Donoghue would return to the role after Ricky's run was over.)

"I saw Tom and two understudies, and after about ten times I closed my eyes and ran the scene through my head as if I were doing it," he explains.

Ricky was completely focused on smoothly stepping into the role because, in his mind, "I have a jewel in my hand, and I don't want to waste it."

The musical *Les Misérables*, which Martin claims "is, I would say, my favorite story," was adapted from the classic book by French poet, novelist, and playwright Victor Hugo, whom Ricky calls "a genius." The story is one of love, obsession, and, finally, redemption—a story so universal that Martin notes, "I believe my theatrical debut in New York could not have been more interesting."

The action takes place in the early nineteenth century. After being imprisoned for nineteen years, working hard labor for stealing some food, Jean Valjean discovers that the yellow ticket-of-leave he must, by law, display condemns him to be an outcast. Only the saintly Bishop of Digne treats him kindly, but Valjean, embittered by years of hardship, responds to the kindness by stealing some of the bishop's silver.

Jean is apprehended by the police, but when asked, the bishop covers for Valjean and tells the officers he gave the candlesticks to him as a gift. That simple act of kindness prompts Jean to turn his life around.

Eight years pass. Valjean now goes by the name Monsieur Madeleine. Although he has built a stellar reputation, owning a factory and serving as mayor of his town, Montreuil-sur-Mer, Jean is also a wanted criminal for having broken his parole all those years ago.

When the other workers find out that their coworker, the beautiful Fantine, has borne a secret, illegitimate child, the other women demand she leave. And when Fantine rejects the advances of her landlord, he throws her out.

Because Fantine desperately needs medicine for her daughter, Cosette, she sells the only things of value she owns—her locket, her hair, and, finally, herself. But even that ends in failure when she gets into a fight with a prospective customer and ends up being arrested. But before the policeman Javert can have her taken away to jail, Valjean, as mayor, intervenes, and insists she be taken to a hospital.

Because Valjean has gone over Javert's head, the policeman begins to watch the mayor closely. Then one day, as Jean lifts a cart off a man pinned beneath it, Javert begins to suspect the mayor is not who he seems. Watching the show of strength brings to mind prisoner 24601, Jean Valjean—a parole breaker whom Javert tracked for years before recently claiming to have found him. When Jean finds out another man may be sentenced for his crimes, he confesses to the court that he is prisoner 24601.

Meanwhile, at the hospital where Fantine lays dying, Valjean promises he will look after her daughter Cosette. And just as Javert arrives to arrest him, Valjean escapes and goes to find the young girl, who has been staying with an abusive family named the Thénardiers at their inn. In her time there, Cosette has known only hardship, while the Thénardiers' own daughter, Eponine, lives like a princess. When Valjean arrives, he pays the Thénardiers to let him take Cosette away, and together they leave for Paris, with Jean knowing full well Javert will never stop hunting him.

Nine years pass. It is 1832 and Paris is a hotbed of unrest, as the city's poor rail against governmental disinterest. Everywhere one looks, there seem to be children roaming the street unsupervised, often in gangs intent on thievery. One of the street gangs is led by the innkeeper Thénardier and his wife, who attack Jean and Cosette one night. But Valjean and the girl are rescued by none other than Javert, who does not recognize Valjean until Jean has quickly sneaked out of sight. One of the student revolutionaries, Marius, witnesses everything, then enlists the help of the Thénardiers' daughter Eponine to help find Cosette, with whom he has fallen in love from afar. Although Eponine is secretly in love with Marius, she agrees to help.

Marius belongs to a student group that is prepared for revolution, which they believe is inevitable once General Lamarque, an advocate for the city's poor, dies. When Gavroche, a street urchin, brings the news of the general's death, the students, led by Enjolras, stream out into the streets to whip up popular support. But Marius's political fervor is suddenly dissipated by thoughts of Cosette.

Likewise, Cosette is obsessed by thoughts of Marius, with whom she has fallen in love. Valjean realizes that his daughter is growing up but can't bring himself to tell her the truth about the past. While Jean agonizes over what to do, Eponine brings Marius to Valjean's house and in the process prevents her father's gang from robbing it. Jean, however, assumes it was Javert lurking outside and abruptly decides he and Cosette must leave France immediately.

On the eve of the revolution, Cosette and Marius part in despair of ever meeting again, Eponine mourns the loss of Marius, while Valjean looks forward to the security of exile. The Thénardiers, meanwhile, dream of robbing everyone blind once the chaos of revolution begins. Eponine, who has joined with the students, takes Cosette a letter from Marius, which Jean intercepts. But despite his warnings, Cosette leaves to join her love where they are building a barricade against the troops to come, giving Jean no choice but to follow.

Chaos ensues. Gavroche exposes Javert as a police spy, and as she tries to rejoin the revolutionaries, Eponine is shot and killed. Valjean arrives at the barricades in search of Marius. There he confronts Javert, but instead of killing him, lets him go.

As the new day dawns, the students' ammunition is running low, and when Gavroche runs out to get more, he is shot. In the end, all the revolutionaries are killed. The sole survivor is Marius, and Valjean carries the unconscious student to safety via the city sewers.

But when he climbs out of the sewers into the light, he is confronted by Javert. No longer concerned about his own safety, Jean pleads with Javert to let him take Marius to the hospital and then he will surrender willingly.

In a shocking turnaround, Javert decides to let Valjean go. Javert's rigid belief that the law is everything has been destroyed by Valjean's mercy. Unable to live after his whole belief system has been shattered, Javert commits suicide by falling into the rushing River Seine and drowning.

Meanwhile, Marius recovers in Cosette's care, unaware that Jean is the one who saved his life. Valjean confesses the truth of his past to Marius. Jean insists that after the young couple are married, he must go away and let them live in peace without the cloud of his past hanging over them rather than taint the sanctity and safety of their union.

At their wedding, Marius discovers through the Thénardiers that it was Valjean who rescued him that night. He and Cosette immediately go to Jean, where Cosette finally learns of her own history. Now completely unburdened, Jean Valjean dies, joining the spirits of Fantine, Eponine, and all those who died on the barricades.

The theatricality and passion of *Les Misérables* appealed to the depths of Ricky's own passionate soul. And facing a new challenge made the adrenaline rush through his body at full fury.

"I've met all the great theater people, which is fantastic! And every night you have a tough crowd and you have to win them over," he noted. "It's very unpredictable, and that's just what I wanted. I don't want an audience that's going to love everything I do, no matter what it is."

It didn't take long for Ricky to win the theater crowds over and to help introduce theater to a generation of Latin youths who might have never considered going to see a musical except for Ricky's presence in the role of the idealistic French revolutionary.

When Ricky made his debut, he was the tenth Marius in

the long-running Broadway production and was appearing during the tenth anniversary of the show's opening. By the enthusiastic applause and heavy sighing when he sang, Ricky's fans were in evidence everywhere the night of his debut. When the show ended, the cheers were let loose as he made his very first curtain call, or, as he called it, "I am going to make my house."

Also in the theater that night were Ricky's beaming parents, Enrique Martin and Nerieda Morales, who flew in from San Juan to see their son's Broadway debut. Also in the house were gaggles of *General Hospital* fans, hoping to get their fix of Ricky Martin, who had left the soap earlier that year. And Ricky's big moments—the second act solo, "Empty Chairs at Empty Tables" and "A Little Fall of Rain," which he sings as Eponine dies in his arms—left his family teary-eyed and proud and fans wanting more.

And left Ricky feeling as if there were nothing he couldn't accomplish if he put his mind to it.

Ricky hits the beach.

(All photos by Ramey Photo Agency)

Ricky poses for the camera.

Thinking about the future.

Pedal to the metal.

Getting ready
to go downhill.

In need of a hug.

Angel
on a
Harley.

The
future's
so bright,
I gotta
wear
shades.

"Easy Rider."

Ricky relaxes.

Hunk at home.

Care to join me?

Call me.

Music and the Music Maker.

Animal lover.

Here's looking at you.

The perfect smile.

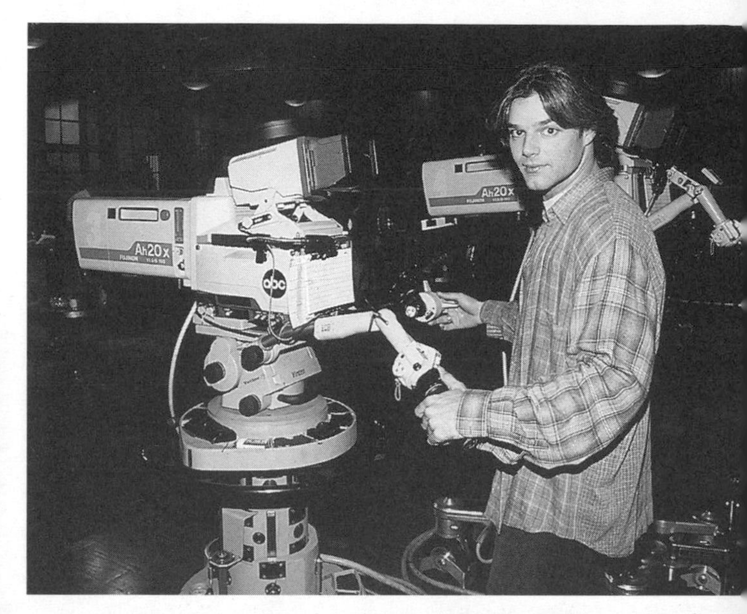

Behind the camera at "General Hospital".

Joking around with Lynn Herring and John J. York on the set of "General Hospital".

With ex-Menudo buddy, Robi Rosa.

On the set
of the
"Hercules"
video.

Tall, dark and handsome.

Getting ready to hit the stage at Whittier Narrows Park in Los Angeles.

On stage before a live audience.

What's next?

9

Back in the Recording Studio

Ricky was contracted to stay with *Les Misérables* through the summer until September 8, 1996. But once he wrapped his run with the musical, rather than take a brief rest to recoup from the rigors of doing eight shows a week, he was scheduled to leave almost immediately on yet another concert tour—which included stops in Miami, Hawaii, Texas, Phoenix, New Mexico, San Francisco, San Diego, and Los Angeles—while also preparing to start recording his fourth album that October.

Some fans wondered if Ricky would include any covers of his *Les Misérables* songs, but he downplayed the possibility. "This music is a sound I admire," he said of the Claude-Michel Schönberg compositions in the musical. "And I may do something similar to it. But pop and the Latin rhythms are so important for me and who I am that I will mostly stay with them."

It was somewhat ironic that Ricky was being asked questions regarding music with classical overtones, because in person he seemed to define the pop sensibility. One reporter described his appearance during an interview as a "taut body clothed in a striped cream silk dress shirt with only one of its buttons fastened for a kind of floppy, flyaway look and boxers that ride above the waist of faded denims." But regardless of his fashion sense, Ricky was a throwback to performers of another era, who conquered music, film, and theater with equal ease.

And like most things he had tried in his life, Ricky's Broadway debut was an unqualified success—which is not to say he didn't have some growing pains. Such as the night he accidentally whacked costar Craig Schulman, who played Jean Valjean, with his sword. At first Ricky was terrified he had hurt Schulman, not to mention embarrassed that he had been careless. But the older actor shrugged the incident off, telling Ricky, "Everyone has his story on the barricades, and this will be your first."

Not only were audiences charmed by Ricky, but so were critics. Said one reviewer:

> *Frankly, he couldn't have picked a better show, or a better role.* Les Misérables *is one of Broadway's class acts, with a powerful book based on the classic Victor Hugo novel, as well as strong songs and solid staging. So a critically successful run in* Les Misérables *carries more credibility than in lighter-fare musicals. Though not the lead, the role of Marius is sizeable and pivotal; yes, it's the romantic role (you had to ask?) and he has several numbers to sing during the course of the three-hour show.*

Although fans seemed to most enjoy Ricky's solo numbers, his personal favorite moment of the production was ''when Jean Valjean is going through a cathartic moment telling me his life at the end of the second act.''

Some fans, however, were disappointed that Ricky as Marius didn't have the opportunity to show off very many dance moves in the musical, although Ricky was happy with his limited choreography. ''If it's a musical you get to dance, too, so you're in touch with a lot of different aspects of performing.''

Such as singing. And for those who came to hear his voice, they were amply rewarded. There aren't many pop or rock stars who could tackle the musical demands of the *Les Misérables* score, but Ricky, despite not being classically trained, managed to handle his musical numbers solidly.

But Ricky said much of the credit went to his costars. ''I never felt alone working with the actors that have been doing this show for many years. The director did an outstanding job. But at the same time I was so hungry for that role. It didn't cause any trauma. I would do this role *any*time. And working with incredible performers. I've learned a lot from them.''

Such as how to get it right the first time. ''In theater, if you miss . . . you miss!'' explains Ricky. ''On TV you can cut and start the scene again. Also, in theater it's always different, every night. The audience has a lot to do with it.''

Ricky also said he learned that the most important part of doing theater was discipline. ''It's very important. Doing a show like *Les Miz*, eight shows a week, it is exhausting. So you need to rest a lot and take singing lessons regularly.''

Punctuality was important, too. ''I have to be there at

seven-thirty. Because if you show up at seven-thirty-three then you get a memo and you'll get in trouble!''

One of the best parts of doing *Les Misérables* was the chance for Ricky to spend time once more in New York City, although this time as a working actor. Like most performers in his position, he loved Manhattan's nonstop energy.

''New York City is a city with a great personality,'' he enthused. ''It inspired me a lot to write my music just sitting on a bench in the park and looking at people's faces.''

But sometimes little hints would creep in that Ricky was perhaps beginning to get a little overloaded, such as an incident that occurred when members of his Los Angeles fan club flew to New York to see Martin in *Les Misérables.* Although they thoroughly enjoyed the performance, they were left shocked and disappointed when Ricky didn't show up for a planned fan lunch.

As someone who had always cherished his fans and went out of his way to recognize and thank them, Ricky was horrified at the faux pas. ''First of all, I apologize,'' he went on record as saying. ''It was a terrible misunderstanding—I had no knowledge about the lunch.'' Ricky was so disturbed, in fact, at the thought that these fans might have been left disappointed that he promised to make arrangements for another function as soon as he returned to Los Angeles.

But for the most part, troubling moments such as that were rare for Ricky, who otherwisc was enjoying himself immensely as the new talk of New York. Suddenly it seemed as if everybody wanted a little piece of Ricky. He was swamped with interview requests—not only did newspapers want to talk to him; television shows were also knocking at his door. One of his first appearances was on Ricki Lake's show.

"I had a lot of fun," Ricky said. "I always have a lot of fun on those shows. Although I would like to do more shows where I can talk more about myself and my concerns as an entertainer as well as a human being."

The summer of 1996 passed quickly, and almost before he knew it, Ricky's final night in *Les Misérables* arrived. It was a bittersweet experience going out for his final curtain call, and he knew that no matter what happened in the rest of his career, having starred on Broadway would always be one of the highlights of what had been an eventful couple of years. Although not everything had worked out the way he had hoped. The biggest disappointment had been the failure of his television pilot, *Barefoot in Paradise,* to be picked up as a series.

"The story was horrible," Ricky admits. "But Zalman King did a great job as a director."

But it was really a minor setback. And as he stood poised to begin work on his next album and turn his attentions fully back to his music, Ricky evaluated what having been on *General Hospital* and in *Les Misérables* had meant to him personally and professionally.

While some actors regarded daytime dramas as also-rans when compared to prime time or films, to Ricky it had been an important and welcome opportunity.

"Who could complain about having spent an hour a day for years on American television? To be able to introduce myself and become known was great. Even today, after not having been on the show for a while, I meet people on the street who ask me when I will return.

They didn't kill me, so that means that I can come back. Of course, even if they *did* kill me, I could still come back!'' Ricky joked, before adding seriously, ''But I don't believe that I'll do it. I think that, modesty aside, I am at another level now.''

Which meant that Ricky was also less inclined to do another *novela* for Latin American television, although he couldn't rule it out completely. ''I don't know. It would have to be something well done, where I could write part of the script. There would be many conditions.

''I am one of those people who fights hard for the public to demand more from artists, and sometimes the material that you are given is not defensible in that aspect. That is why I refuse to do things I don't believe in, although I should say that I have been fortunate, because I have not had the economic necessity to do anything that I don't like. In any event, I will continue fighting and being demanding of myself.''

Whether or not he would return to the world of American soaps, Ricky would forever be grateful for all the opportunities *General Hospital* had afforded him and for the friends he had made there. ''Yes. Especially Lilly Melgar and Kimberly McCullough.'' He got to see the latter quite a bit during his theater run because she was living in New York then, studying art at NYU.

Not surprisingly, though, he raved most about *Les Misérables*. ''I left *General Hospital* because I had the opportunity to do Broadway, and that was a lifelong dream. I made it to Broadway, which is something so lovely. I have made a quantum leap in my career.''

For all the other doors it opened for Ricky, it had fulfilled his ultimate goal of combining his passion for music with his love of acting. "When I do both, it's like paradise to me. I think I grew a lot as an entertainer. I grew a lot as a person.

"It was fascinating to deal with classical sounds and a very difficult audience in front of you. People who go to my concert more or less know what's going to happen, and they are more or less familiar with who I am. But in the play, every night I had to sweat to get the standing ovation, and at the end of the show if you don't get the standing ovation, it's the most frustrating thing you can feel. Of course, it never happened," he said with a laugh.

Despite the exhilarating experience, Ricky surprised some by making it clear he wouldn't necessarily rush into another Broadway production. "What happens is that when one begins with *Les Misérables,* one cannot go back. Of course I will never say never, but if I return in another classic, I would like to be part of the original cast. There's nothing on paper yet, but hopefully, one day, yes.

"The bottom line is, if they offered me something that was important for me, I would do it. I won't close off that possibility because, of course, once you do theater it becomes kind of addictive and you have to do it again. It is one of the most beautiful things I've done in my life. Just being able to sing, dance, and act and have the audience with you at the same time!

"And I'm going to keep working on my studies as an actor. Because I really want to do film here in the States or in Europe."

But the fact was, Ricky wasn't even sure when he'd go back to acting of any kind. "Tomorrow maybe I'll go back into acting,'' he said, but in his heart, it was time to immerse himself once more in music.

''I love the music behind me and the fans' reaction. That's the ultimate pleasure for me. Even when I've been doing acting, I've been doing music. There has always been something on the radio from Ricky Martin. Even when I was doing *General Hospital* and I was locked in a television studio for hours, you know, with the hurry-up-and-wait kind of thing? When I had two hours I would go into the studio and I would record and I would send something to the radio for them to be playing. I needed that.''

With the ambitious schedule Ricky had lined up for himself, he would be getting double doses of his music fix well into the then-foreseeable future. After finishing up his fourth Spanish language album, Ricky of course would tour, but then he intended to make the leap into mainstream American music.

''I will be releasing an English album next spring, hopefully in March,'' he announced in late 1996. He admitted to having some nervousness about doing his first English-language album. ''With Spanish being my first language, it's naturally more comfortable. But I love challenges, so singing in English, or any other language, is a rush.''

The one thing he wouldn't be doing anytime soon was reuniting with his former Menudo mates for a reunion record or tour, which had been suggested as a possibility.

''Menudo was a great experience and a great beginning. The best school possible. But now my dreams are different and I'm doing everything I can to realize them. Today I would say no, but then again, in the future you never know!''

But for Ricky, the future was now.

10

On Tour

Although Ricky had experienced the surround-sound fan intensity, for some reason it was magnified now because it was all directed solely at him. If the crowds had been adoring before, after *A Medio Vivir* they became positively slavishly devoted. In country after country, Ricky was the heartthrob to beat. His tour for that album, *Fuego de Noche, Nieve de Día*, began in Puerto Rico, then traveled to Mexico, through parts of America, and on to Europe and the Middle East.

The American leg of the tour was in large part to promote his ''Spanglish'' version of ''Maria,'' which was then playing on American crossover stations.

As of the end of September and beginning of October, Ricky would be going to Rio de Janeiro to do a concert. His song ''Maria'' would also be featured as the theme song in the hit Brazilian soap opera *Salsa y Merengue*. From Brazil, Ricky was scheduled to continue on to Spain, where he would perform in various cities, including Madrid and Barcelona, and then continue on to Lisbon, Portugal.

But it wasn't a case of following a straight touring line. Because of the vagaries of scheduling a multination concert tour, Ricky found himself zigzagging the globe, flying back and forth between continents at a dizzying pace.

In October 1996, Ricky performed in Spain, then hopped a jet to Miami, where he appeared at the James Knight Center for a star-studded event for TV5, the Spanish television channel. In addition to Ricky, the other performers included Latin music stars such as Miguel Bose, Laura Pausini, and Azúcar Moreno. The concert was broadcast live to Spain, and Ricky was asked to perform two songs, "Te Extraño" and, of course, "Maria," which left the Miami crowd literally begging for more.

In fact, the crowds got so raucous and large that extra security had to be called in out of fear the fans might get out of control, as happened once to the young stars of *Beverly Hills 90210* at the height of their popularity.

From south Florida, Martin flew back up to New York, where he appeared on October 13 at Madison Square Garden along with Enrique Iglesias, Marcos Llunas, Paulina Rubio, and Los Del Rio in a concert hosted by Suave Radio 93.1, a popular Latin radio station in New York.

This time, Ricky was onstage much longer, performing nine songs and once again bringing the house to its feet and knees simultaneously. Sadly for Ricky, it was his last scheduled American concert for the year because now he was off to sing to the world, flying directly to Brazil, where he spent a full week performing in Rio de Janeiro and São Paolo.

From there, Ricky and his band headed for Ecuador, Chile, Peru, and Argentina, one after the other. During this time, life was a series of getting on and off planes, catching sleep wherever and whenever possible. However, Argentina would prove to be particularly special, because that was the site of the biggest concert in Ricky's solo performing career.

"At the Buenos Aires concert, two hundred and seventy-five thousand people were there," Ricky says.

His concert not only shattered the attendance record held by Pavarotti, but highlighted the danger that can come with even the most well-meaning of fans when too many people gather in one spot. Over four hundred people had to be helped away from the concert by the Argentinian Red Cross for ailments and injuries related to the overcrowding, but luckily nobody was seriously hurt.

However, intent on preventing any harm coming to Ricky or the members of his band, concert promoters assigned a special security detail to Ricky, the likes of which are often reserved for political figures.

"After that show in Argentina, I was depressed. Isn't it ironic? You know, the biggest show you've ever done and you get a little sad."

But Ricky had little time to indulge his emotions because the road continued to beckon relentlessly, and he strove on, fueled by his ambition and his passion for performing. Immediately following his stunning Argentina success, Ricky flew back to Spain to perform the second series of concerts in two months, this time appearing in Madrid, Seville, and Barcelona, and Ricky was already swimming in a sea of interview requests from all the different Spanish media.

Considering that when he wasn't singing, Ricky seemed to be talking to magazine, newspaper, or television reporters, it's amazing he had any voice left. However, his schedule did allow his the briefest of breaks after his Spanish tour. He was able to lay over in New York for several days before gearing back up and flying down to Mexico for several days of concerts.

Not that his time in New York was spent relaxing. While there Ricky filmed the video for his next single, "Bon Bon de Azúcar," which, like "Maria" and "Qué Día Es Hoy" before it, would be remixed for radio play. Because all his songs were in Spanish, American video networks such as MTV and VH-1 didn't play his music videos, but, as he noted, "MTV Latino has "Maria" and "Fuego de Noche, Nieve de Día" in the top ten right now. MTV Europe also," he added proudly.

Also getting airplay on the Spanish stations was "Diana," a duet Ricky recorded with Paul Anka. But Ricky had little time to reflect on everything happening in his career because he was leaving again, this time for south of the border. However, he seemed completely unfazed by the unrelenting travel and appearances.

"If I had to stop working for several weeks, I think I would go crazy. I need to work; I really love what I'm doing. Three weeks, that's too long. When I've had a month off and they'd ask me to stay for one week more, I think I'd start to panic!"

The highlight of the Mexican leg of the tour was his November 16 appearance at the Palacio de Deportes in Mexico City for the Radio Pulsar all-day festival. Once again, Ricky joined a stellar lineup of Latin musical talent, such as Enrique Iglesias, Miguel Bose, Jaguares, Chayanne, Laura Pausini, Alejandro Fernandez, and Mana. And once again, it was Ricky who ignited the crowd, closing his two-song set with a remixed version of "Maria."

With the cheers of the crowd still ringing in his ears, Ricky found himself winging back across the Atlantic for two more weeks of concerts, including a visit to Scandinavia, Portugal, and Germany, where "Maria" was burning up the charts, proving that even in countries where Spanish was not the predominant language, Ricky could be a huge crossover success.

Despite the almost superhuman demands of touring, Ricky never complained or acted the prima donna.

"It's true, my career *is* very hectic. But I always look back on how it all began. I see myself as a poor little boy with big dreams. And I ask myself, 'Is this little boy proud of what he has made and what he has become?' Up till now this little boy is very happy and feels he's on the right track. It gives me the motivation to keep going and prevents me from getting lazy. Besides, success might be over before you know it."

Possible, but not likely for Ricky. However, there were one or two places on earth he could still go and not be mobbed, and being in those situations was good for his perspective on stardom.

"I went on a promotion trip to Switzerland and in the evening we went to a club. And nobody had ever heard of Ricky Martin. It was a neat and strange feeling. But to be honest, the loss of a private life is a toll this career takes on you. On the other hand, it gives me many advantages. If it had been important to me to be able to buy bread without being recognized, I would have become a teacher or worked in an office. I wanted it to be like it is now," he says in a refreshing change from so many millionaire stars who resent being bothered by the very fans who made them famous.

"I can't wait to be recognized in the United States," said Ricky. "Being recognized in the street doesn't bother me; otherwise, I'd wear a disguise. In a city like New York, life is easy. New Yorkers are used to seeing stars who are far more important than I am walking across the street. They can meet actors like Robert De Niro or Al Pacino, so who's Ricky Martin?" he says with self-deprecating modesty.

In December 1996, Ricky was scheduled to go back to America and begin work on his two new album projects. Finally he was able to stop, take a deep breath, and evaluate the previous several months, which had been nothing short of amazing.

While in Argentina, Ricky had received several gold and platinum record awards on behalf of *A Medio Vivir*. One of the biggest topics of conversation among the Argentinian media was the news that Ricky had grown a beard and was wearing his hair shorter.

His appearances in Spain had been so well received that he was scheduling another series of concerts for the summer of 1997 there. As soon as the dates were announced, the tickets were sold, prompting the promoters to request even more shows. Ricky's album, already in the top twenty, surged upward to seventh on the charts after his visit.

By far, the most successful song of the *A Medio Vivir* album was "Maria," which kept going and going like the Energizer Bunny. For almost two years "Maria" was being played in rotation on some radio station in one part of the world or another, because wherever the song was released, it was a smash hit.

As evidence of the song's immense popularity, two different videos of it were made, the second shot in Paris while Ricky was in France on tour. Ricky was unabashed in admitting how much he loved the City of Lights.

"I love to walk by the River Seine, and I love the architecture of Paris, too. I went to the Louvre," he says, referring to the world-famous art museum, "and I can't wait to go back again.

"If I wanted to spend ten thousand francs within the hour, I'd run off to Montmartre and I'd buy a painting from one of the painters on the 'place du Tertre.' I'd be so happy to constantly have that corner of Paris I love so much.

"I'd really like to spend a day in Paris all by myself. Just go into the first park I see. Do nothing, contemplate, sit on a bench and watch the people going by. For me, the guy who never takes a break, that would be the greatest luxury. Three years ago, I'd do that sort of thing, often on my birthday on December twenty-fourth. And nothing could have made me happier."

Of course, it's not surprising that Ricky, the romantic idol, loves the ultimate city of romance. Unfortunately, though, he lamented at the time that he was in Paris at a time when he was single, with no special woman in his life.

"A year ago I almost got married," he said in an interview while on tour. "But when I saw myself buying a ring inside a jewelry store, I got scared and I changed my mind. I didn't know what I was doing there, and I had clearly realized that it wasn't my moment."

Naturally, his romantic experiences, particularly the ones that don't end as happily as expected, end up in his music.

"Most of my songs are inspired by personal experiences. Like everyone, I've known the pangs of love. Life is full of highs and lows. After breaking up, luckily there are always reconciliation and rebirth. But if everything went perfectly all the time, it would get pretty boring, wouldn't it? I think it's very important to give the audience a piece of sincerity.

"The audience doesn't always want to swim in pink, in the unreal, in fantasy," Ricky adamantly believes. "They need reality, they need to listen to stories that resemble their experiences. If people want to change their ideas for a perfect illusion, then they should go and watch some sitcom or something that is fiction! On the other hand, in music, I think it's better to use the rhythm of the heart, feelings, real emotions!"

Although Ricky readily admits he has nothing against fun, playful sex—"Of course, who doesn't like that? It's about creation here."—he prefers the sensual side of romance.

"My background is very sensual, and when I say my background is my music, my people, it's very passionate. The dancing is passionate. If you listen to the biggest hits of Latin America, like lambada, they're very sensual movements, and it's a way of living. If you go to the Carnival in Rio, people will be like, 'Oh, my God, the lady's naked. Oh, my God, they're touching each other!' But that's the way of living. That's the way it is. There are no taboos when it comes to—people call it sex, but it's a way of living. That's the way it is, and I can't erase that from my blood; it comes with it.

"But," he adds, "I'm still a gentleman, and I respect who my girlfriend is or other people's background because they can get a little bit intimidated with that. So I don't walk into a place strutting my stuff, if you know what I mean. Because that's not me either."

Despite all the hot Latin blood coursing through his veins, Ricky says he's really rather old-fashioned in many respects, although accepting of others' lifestyles.

"I consider myself someone kind of conservative when it comes to sex. But I'm not judgmental either. I'm talking about myself, I'm talking to straight, gay, lesbian, it doesn't matter. Life is too short not to be happy. You've got to be happy. If you're happy making love to a dog, go for it," he jokes. "No, don't do that, don't do that. But seriously, even though my background could be so moral, still there is that mix of not judging, and I give a lot of credit to my background because of that."

It's ironic that of all countries in which to film his video, France was chosen, because that's the one language he has trouble with.

"I love languages. I speak almost five. I'm fluent in Spanish and Portuguese, English, Italian, and French but French has been the hardest because of the accent. But I can understand it and read it—I just have to work on my accent to get it right."

Ricky also further endeared himself to the French by waxing poetic about homegrown singing star Vanessa Paradis.

"I dream of doing a duet with Vanessa Paradis!" Ricky said enthusiastically. "Vanessa is a beautiful girl. She's loaded with talent. I admire her work, but also her beauty. She fascinates me—even simply because she's a woman. In fact, I admire all women because they have the ability to give birth to a child. It's an incredible feat!''

It seemed everywhere he went, Ricky managed to leave a charmed country in his wake. And as his popularity grew, Ricky became more than just a performer; he became a marketable commodity as well.

11

Ricky Style!

It's a reflection of Ricky's personality that he is often drawn to countries where his popularity was tepid. Whereas some performers' egos couldn't bear not being all the rage, for Ricky it became a personal challenge to win them over, which is what he did when visiting the Netherlands.

"What I find more important than just dropping by now is that in ten years' time I can come back and still get the Dutch people dancing or get them into a romantic mood with my music," he explained in an interview. "I know I'm not very popular here yet and I know I have to work hard, but I don't mind that.

"I also know that there are always artists appearing who have one big hit and you'll never see them again. But I don't want to be like that. I don't want to be dramatic, but this is my career, my life, my all!"

One thing Ricky has going for him is that even though he is the darling of the women, guys like him, too. "I do tend to attract that type of audiences, yes, but my fans are very varied. Women, women with their boyfriends or husbands, men by themselves—the ages vary a lot, too, from about sixteen to thirty-five.''

The other appeal of traveling in a country where Rickymania didn't exist was that he had more freedom just to be himself, instead of having his every move regulated by security because he was being followed by mobs of fans.

''Yes, that happens regularly, in places like Argentina, Mexico, and Brazil. Sometimes I sneak past the security and leave my hotel. I go in disguise with a hat on or something like that and I go walking or cycling. If I don't have my bike with me, I rent one. My security guards don't like it, but suddenly they'll see me riding past them and I'll give them a friendly wave, like: I did it again!''

For as much as he thrived on performing, Ricky did pay a heavy price when it came to his personal life—as in, he didn't have one.

''I have hardly any private life! I know it's a part of it and there's nothing to be done about it. It's a bit of a double standard; I want to be famous but I want some privacy as well. But I'm not as obsessed with this as I used to be. There's no sense in trying to change things that you can't change. It's better to keep myself busy with things I *can* influence.''

And in that regard, Ricky was very aware of the power of celebrity and felt a responsibility to use it wisely and not let it all go to his head. ''I'm just being myself, and that's really the best way.''

It seemed as if Ricky spent a lot of time trying to convince others that he really wasn't taken with himself and that he didn't spend all day primping in front of the mirror.

"No, not at all," he says emphatically. "The people who work with me are always in charge of taking care of my skin and my hair. They want to apply creams and treatments on me, but they get annoyed because I ignore them. I like to look good, but I like to look good naturally. I always go to the gym and I enjoy lifting weights and doing exercises."

Ricky will, however, admit to occasional bouts of vanity. "Sometimes. It depends on what I have to do on a certain day. Look, I can't go onto the stage looking like a tramp. So in the morning I can take a long time to get ready, but if I have a day off, then I keep it simple—I take a shower, then throw on socks, trousers, shirt, shoes, do a quick job on the hair, and Ricky's ready!"

Ricky also reveals that he's a traditionalist when it comes to underwear! "One thing I won't wear is red underwear! I think that's really the worst thing there is. I just wear white. Virgin white. 'Cause I'm a good boy! Yes," he teases, "good boys do exist!"

Unmentionables aside, Ricky *does* have his own sense of style, depending upon "how I get up. I'm never following the dictated fashion." He likes his hair, for example, which gets hot, messy. "My hair used to be very long before, down to my shoulders, and that was good for a while. Next time, though, it might be Kojak!

"But it's very important to know what's happening in the fashion industry." And Ricky would later get the opportunity to keep tabs on the current trends up close and personal when designer Giorgio Armani recruited him to be a model.

"I had never done modeling before when he asked me to. He just gives me the clothes and I wear them. I really do like fashion. I like to know what's happening. It's a personality thing, not because I'm in the music business. I would like fashion even if I wasn't in show business.''

But the fact was, fashion was important to him because of his concert show, which some described as a fashion parade, with Ricky changing clothes up to five times over the course of the show. When onstage, he was partial to suits, sweaters, and shirts in a variety of fabrics, mostly silk, linen, and velvet.

Just as Ricky was attentive to fashion, he was equally attentive to fitness and being healthy. Unlike other singers, who spend most of their time on the road drinking or doing drugs, Ricky's body is a clean-living temple.

''I'm a totally sober kind of man,'' he declares. ''I don't even drink wine. At this moment of my life, I desire and need as much peace and calm as possible, and drugs represent the total opposite. I even quit smoking two years ago.''

Despite his obvious personal discipline, Ricky says there are still plenty of areas in his life that need improvement.

''There are a lot of things about myself I would like to change. I have the tendency to be influenced too easily. If you ask me, the last person who spoke was right.

''And I'd like to be less vulnerable, less fragile, less affected by the things that hurt me. I have a lot of pain. The two things that get to me most are hypocrisy and cynicism. Also, I'm not the kind of person who wants to hide his emotions, but I've always wanted to protect those things I love from being made public without consent.

''As I always say, I don't sell my room keys. What I

sell are the tickets for my shows, so sometimes I do wish I could live like everybody else.''

But destiny dictated otherwise, and Ricky adjusted the best he could. One way of keeping himself centered was to maintain strong ties to his native island.

''My family's my balance. My friends are the ones I had at school,'' Ricky notes, adding that his fantasy would be to ''bring my friends on the road. I speak to my family a lot, though. My whole family lives in Puerto Rico. I live in Miami now, but Puerto Rico is still my home; it's just that my house is in Miami.''

Like the house he owned while living in Los Angeles, Ricky's Miami residence is decorated in a very tasteful, understated way so that it is a light, airy retreat from the world.

On the rare occasions he's home, Ricky says he mostly ''sleeps, sleeps, and sleeps again. I shut myself up in my house in Miami and relax. I read books, send for a pizza, listen to music, call my friends—really unspectacular and normal things. I often seek silence!''

Martin says it's not unusual for him to wake up early and just stay in his room to ''enjoy the silence. This life is so crazy, it's very hectic, surrounded by a lot of people, the traveling—things can get off balance. For me the best medicine is to talk to myself.''

Writing was also therapeutic for Ricky, who contributed songs to his fourth album, which was recorded in New York and Miami in late 1997. Although Ricky would not dream of turning his back on the catchy rhythms that distinguished his musical sound, he still approached being a songwriter from a serious viewpoint.

''It's important. I write my music for people who are

willing to create a cultural exchange. I write my music for people who are willing to hear about problems in society,'' he says.

Although he didn't necessarily feel under pressure to outdo himself, Ricky was aware that it would be a challenge to match, much less surpass, the impact of *A Medio Vivir*. Or to produce a single that could match ''Maria,'' which had worldwide sales of over four million copies. So instead he simply concentrated on producing the best album he could and would let the fans be the final judge.

The time in the studio was a needed break for Ricky, who would once again schedule an ambitious slate of concerts to promote the disc. Ironically, as Ricky worked on his album, several other former members of Menudo had reunited under the name El Reencuentro, and were also preparing to hit the concert trail.

Enough longtime Menudo fans wondered aloud, in magazines and in Internet chat rooms, why Ricky didn't join them for at least a few concerts, that he took the time to address the issue, albeit briefly.

''It's fantastic that they've come back together after all these years,'' he said. ''But I only have just enough time for myself; I couldn't do that project, too.''

Ricky's highly anticipated fourth album, *Vuelve* (*Come Back*) was released in early 1998, and it was instantly devoured by his fans. And while ''Maria'' would forever be his signature song for many, his new single, ''La Copa de la Vida'' (''The Cup of Life'') was giving ''Maria'' a run for its money.

And as Ricky's profile rose, so did his demand. He was sent movie scripts and television shows, but he refused to rush into anything.

"I wouldn't want to be a star of a film," he said, surprising many. "I want a good part, and that's all I want. I can have a five-minute part—just make those five minutes mine and make them very intense." However, if he *were* in a movie, he admitted he would love to work with Isabella Rossellini and Juliette Binoche.

But for the time being, Ricky was intent on his music. "I need the immediate reaction I get from performing my music, and I'm going to take care of it like it was my baby."

Now in addition to all the interviews, concerts, and promotional personal appearances that consumed his time, Martin was also the new golden boy of advertisers, including international companies such as Pepsi. So in addition to traveling the world singing, Ricky was now jet-setting to star in commercials, such as the one he filmed in Italy for Suzuki, the motorcycle manufacturer.

To his credit, Ricky approached every job—whether it was an acting role, a stage performance, a concert, or a commercial—with equal enthusiasm and commitment. The commercial was shot in the southern part of the country at the Gulf of Naples, in rolling countryside filled with olive trees and jasmine, adjacent to the beach.

Unlike Milan, Rome, or the other congested urban areas of the country, this area is more rural, so the producers didn't have to worry about Ricky starting a mob scene during filming. In part of the commercial, Ricky is seen driving his Suzuki along a winding road, wearing a helmet and sunglasses. Although there were no crowds of lovestruck girls following him around, he had fans in the crew, and after filming was finished for the day, someone popped a tape of *Vuelve* in a player, and Ricky heard himself singing.

Although Ricky isn't a frequent motorcyclist, he handled the bike easily, with no fear. "I'm not really afraid of anything. Skydiving is okay, though I've never done it. But jumping into the sea from a boat at night? No—that would be scary!"

The premise for the commercial has Ricky, as himself, traveling through a small Italian town, when he sees a beautiful girl and becomes enchanted by her. She, however, seems uninterested and disappears from sight. That's when he hops on the Suzuki and chases after his elusive dream woman. Eventually he catches her—this is Italy, after all—and the commercial ends with Ricky and the woman in an embrace.

"The character Sophia plays," he says of his costar, "is comparable to the Maria from my song. She plays with men, but lets no one come closer."

Just as he had in France, Ricky fell in love with Italy, particularly with the people. "The deep religiousness and the family ties here are fantastic," he noted. "You walk down the streets and all of a sudden a mother with ten kids comes along. That's great!"

The subject of family can always make Ricky wistful and sentimental. "I'm a real family man. And when I find the right woman I will marry her. But," he says, "I don't want ten kids. Only three, but I'd love every single one the same. Just like a real Italian mama."

Usually, though, Ricky tends to shy away from questions regarding his love life, such as his relationship with Venezuelan model Rebeca de Alba, about whom Ricky will only say, "Rebeca is someone very special. I understand that a gentleman doesn't talk about his women and respects them. Why make public the person you go out with? No.''

However, he had no qualms talking about his desire to work with popular Australian singer Tina Arena. Ricky and Tina had originally been set to sing the theme song to the Antonio Banderas film *Zorro,* called ''I Want to Spend My Lifetime Loving You.'' But allegedly the deal fell through when Sony wouldn't release Ricky to do it.

But Ricky wasn't deterred. ''I met Tina and worked with her, and she's a great girl. We *will* work together in the future.''

Although as was becoming typical, the issue wasn't what Ricky wanted to do, as much as when he would find the time.

12

The Latin King of Pop

A typical day on tour for Ricky would begin early in the morning and often go until midnight or later, prompting him to admit, "Sometimes I want my days to have forty-eight hours, so I could do more."

What kept him going through the long hours and fatigue was the challenge he had set for himself, the goal to be the best he could be. "If you wish to be different from the others, you have to fight. Nothing is going to come to you for free. If you want to be like everyone else, then take it easy. But if you don't, work hard, work incessantly, and you will eventually stand out over everything and everybody."

Although his primary base of operations was Miami, Ricky owned homes in Puerto Rico, Buenos Aires, and Madrid as well. "It's not a luxury," he insists, aware that to the casual observer it might seem like simple greed to own so many homes.

"What happens is, because I travel so much, I get tired of hotel life. I like to try and feel like home, so I can really rest. And at each house I have my own clothes and my own stuff, so when I travel to these places, I don't need to worry about packing."

However, when he traveled to Asia, he didn't have that particular luxury, so when Ricky and his band came to town, their luggage and equipment could fill a small house.

One major difference between playing Latin America and Asia was the size of the audiences he typically played to. Instead of soccer stadiums that held hundreds of thousands of people, the Asian venues were more intimate, relatively speaking, so the fans felt closer and more a part of the action onstage. What was the same, though, was that just as in Latin America, at every stop he performed, Ricky brought down the house with an act that was polished and sleek.

In Singapore, 4,500 anxious fans gathered at the Harbour Pavilion to watch Ricky perform, many waving Puerto Rican flags. Martin made sure to let them know how much he appreciated their country's hospitality and warmth—especially since the concert started almost an hour late.

"I am going to leave my heart and soul on this stage tonight," he told the crowd. "I hope you do the same, too."

To open the act, Ricky stood motionless in a gray suit as the light shone on him and then got the audience on their feet early with "La Copa de la Vida" and "Maria." Those present were actually making history, because thanks to a change in local law, for the first time concert-goers were being allowed to stand and dance at concerts, and Ricky was the first international star to perform under the new rules. And nobody could have been a better choice in teaching an audience how to move to the music.

His theatricality was evident in the way he assumed different personas over the course of the show—*bolero,* lover, seducer. He also showed his socially conscious side by bringing the audience's attention to the scourge of AIDS, then singing a song written by Brazilian composer Renato Russo, who died of the disease a few years earlier.

In Taipei, Martin was referred to as "the new Latin king of pop." As was his style, he bridged the cultural gap immediately by greeting the audience in Chinese. It has been said a lot that music is a universal language, and perhaps it's never been clearer than with Ricky. Even though his Chinese fans didn't know how to say the Spanish words he was singing, they could still enjoy the moods and rhythms of the music. What they could say, though, and quite clearly and loudly, was his name, and chants of "Ricky! Ricky!" from fourteen thousand fans rang through the air.

Although Ricky had yet to really infiltrate America to a significant degree among Anglos, in Australia, he was wildly popular, much to his admitted amazement. Even after *Vuelve* was released, "Maria" was still being played down under.

" 'Maria' has done so well in Australia, it's amazing. I'm really impressed—I was not ready for what's been happening in Australia. When I got here they gave me the platinum award for it!"

Ricky was on a nonstop schedule, meeting with journalists and appearing on a variety of television programs, including *Red Faces,* a *Gong Show* type of program where people perform their "talent" in front of a panel of celebrity judges.

Ricky proved to have a good sense of humor when he

gave one guy, who wore a blue dress and pink lipstick and sang "Don't Cry for Me, Argentina," a perfect score of ten.

In every country he went, it seemed as if Ricky ended up talking movies, probably because the reporters couldn't believe someone with his matinee-idol looks wasn't a film star.

"I like Australian films because they're a bit more realistic," he said in one interview. "My dream is to play a mentally ill person. My favorite movies are *My Best Friend's Wedding,* and I love *Priscilla, Queen of the Desert.*"

However, the strain of nonstop travel finally caught up with even Ricky, and he ended up having to cut his Australian visit short, returning to Los Angeles to recuperate. Ricky felt so bad at having to cancel that he rescheduled a performance at Sydney's State Theater and at the Palais Theater in Melbourne for later in the year.

Prior to leaving, he had been noticeably weary, and his body finally said, Enough! But as the saying goes, there was little rest for the weary—five days later he was back on a plane for more promotional appearances.

While he was popular in Australia, his reception paled when compared to the fervor he created when traveling to Latin American countries such as Colombia, where he couldn't step out onto the street without donning a disguise. But, he said, the Colombian women and food were too tempting to resist, so he had to risk the crowds.

"Colombian women are an example of the perfect women," he said. And to show he was just as interested in intellect and beauty, he added that one of his favorite books was Gabriel García Márquez's *One Hundred Years of Solitude.*

Arguably, more than any other, Ricky was the most popular young Spanish-language performer in the world, with over fifty smash-hit singles, more than forty of which had been certified as platinum. And his international appeal and ability to connect with people across gender, social, economic, and cultural lines was one reason why his song "La Copa de la Vida" was chosen to be the official song of the 1998 soccer World Cup, and why Ricky was asked to perform it live at the opening ceremonies on July 12 in Paris at the Stade de France prior to the start of the championship game.

But getting Ricky onstage had been tricky because of corporate sponsorships. Ricky is backed by Pepsi, but one of the main sponsors of the World Cup was Coca-Cola. So even though he wanted to participate, Ricky wasn't sure he'd be allowed to. But in the end, Michel Platini, one of the primary organizers of the games, made it happen.

It was an event Ricky would never forget. "At least one billion were watching," he said. "It was a fascinating experience, but I was ready for it because I had been preparing for more than a month. I was just dying to be there. That's the kind of stage I want to go back onto because it's a stage where you grow up as an entertainer, and it really was a fascinating way to exchange cultures. There were more than a billion people watching me perform my music. My music is my rhythms, my sound, and it's the way I present where I come from.

"The audience was very warm. The reactions and comments from the media, internationally speaking, were very positive. But the first thing I did when I left the stadium was to call my mom to check if I had come through clearly at home. My mom was in tears, so I knew it was a success!''

Ricky was also thrilled to be there because he admits to being ''a big fan, but a bad player. But I just love football,'' as soccer is called outside the United States. ''It was Brazil all the way.''

Of course, Brazil lost to the underdog French team in what was considered an upset. Like all the other Brazilian fans, Ricky was bitterly disappointed, but, he says, ''when I left the stadium and I saw the happiness on the French faces, that was great to see. They deserved to win. I've heard a lot of people say that France paid Brazil to let them win, but Brazil would never have done that. Soccer is like a religion over there! They just didn't play too well. Holland was good, Argentina was pitiful, and let's not talk about Spain. . . .''

The most upsetting circumstance, however, was that Ricky's song almost didn't make it onto the official World Cup album.

''The album had already been recorded and was about to be released when the head honcho called and asked if I wanted to do something for the World Cup,'' Ricky recalls. ''I said yes straightaway, because mixing music and sports is a beautiful thing.'' Fortunately, thanks to some quick studio work, the song made it onto the big-selling release.

''La Copa de la Vida'' is a quintessential Ricky Martin song, with a musical hook—''Ale, Ale, Ale!''—that's impossible not to move to. In fact, it picked up where ''Maria'' left off, and would ultimately prove to be one of the most important songs of his career. Not surprisingly, Ricky had once again recruited K. C. Porter and Robi Rosa to produce it and make it "a fusion of all Latin American rhythms which present my ballads and feelings."

In explaining the meaning of "La Copa de la Vida," Martin says, "The cup of life is fusion. The cup of life is dancing. The cup of life is giving me the opportunity to go and bring my culture to all these different cultures. The cup of life brought me to Asia for the first time."

He goes on to note that the title song of the album *Vuelve*, means "come back." "It's the need for the muse to come back. It is the need for the audience to come back. It is the need to go back to my culture. And it's also a very romantic song. It's a song that is pure Catholic, I must say, for me. This is my life. This is who I am today. This is Ricky Martin."

Another song destined to be a chart winner was "La Bomba." "That song is, how can I put this, is a native sound of where I come from. I am describing a girl that can drive every man crazy and can get us to our knees and beg for mercy. But it's all about dancing and having a good time."

But to some, "La Copa de la Vida" represented even more. In addition to being the official anthem of the 1998 World Cup, the song was also appropriated by Puerto Rico's governor, Pedro Rossello, as the theme song for his political party's effort to have Puerto Rico recognized as America's fifty-first state.

In a speech delivered on July 25 in Guánica, Puerto Rico, during the commemoration of the one-hundredth anniversary of the U.S. invasion of Puerto Rico, Rossello pledged that he would not rest until "the single star of the Puerto Rican flag" was sewn "onto the flag of the great American nation, where it rightfully belongs." During the festivities, "La Copa de la Vida" played unceasingly.

What is ironic is that Ricky has gone on record as saying he is "one hundred percent apolitical."

From dance music to love song back to hip-moving songs, Ricky gave his fans the gamut of musical emotions. And that emotion, as had been proven time and time again, was universal in its appeal. But as was obvious, so was Ricky himself.

In Venezuela, television networks aired specials about Ricky's life, even after his concert was over and he had flown on to his next stop. However, to Ricky, the concert he'd held in Venezuela was special because he had dedicated it to his beloved grandmother, whose picture he still carried, and who had recently died. When he talked about it, it was obvious to those in the audience that he was fighting to keep his emotions under control.

Back in the United States, Ricky performed a Halloween concert at Madison Square Garden and showed off his mastery of English by telling the crowd he would like "to leave his heart and soul. It's a lot of work, but it pays off."

Ricky performed with four backup singers, although his vocals carried the majority of the show, from the ballads to the showstoppers like "Maria" and "La Bomba." His energy was almost superhuman, as he pranced, salsaed, and rumbaed through the performance. The show ended with a display of fireworks and the inflation of giant dancing dolls on the sides of the stage.

When the show was over, Ricky sent the audience off with *"Que Dios los bendiga y la Virgen los acompañe."* ("May God bless you and the Virgin be with you.")

In November, Ricky presided over the grand opening of his own Miami restaurant, Casa Salsa. Located in the fashionable South Beach area, the restaurant would feature authentic Puerto Rican gourmet food.

"I'm going to bring the chef from the Ajilimojili restaurant in Puerto Rico, who prepares scrumptious meals," Martin said. He also planned to offer live music in the back of the restaurant, from salsa to jazz. But of course, Ricky had to leave almost immediately to go back on the road.

Then in December of 1998, it was announced that Ricky was nominated for three Channel V awards held in Delhi, India, where he won Best International Male Artist! He was also nominated for an American Music Award in the Favorite Latin Music Artist category.

With two mega-albums behind him, awards adorning his mantel, and the world at his feet, Ricky was truly ready to confront the biggest challenge of his career—conquering the United States.

"God willing, in 1999 my first album in English will be released," he announced in late 1998. "I hope it will be well received."

Not even the eternally optimistic Ricky Martin could have predicted just how well received he was about to be.

13

Today's Latin Music Scene

Sometimes success is as simple as being in the right place at the right time. Jerry Seinfeld created a concept for a television show poking fun at the "Me Generation" and became a cultural phenomenon. Sylvester Stallone wrote a movie about an underdog during a time when Americans were wondering about their place in the world, and *Rocky* became a cultural phenomenon. Elvis Presley threw off the shackles of the repressed 1950s and became a cultural phenomenon. Of course, the question can be argued, were these performers the ultimate product of their times or did their creative foresight change the times in which they lived?

Nobody's saying that Ricky Martin is the next Seinfeld, Stallone, or Presley, but then again, who knows? What is known is that Latin music is on the brink of exploding into mainstream American consciousness, and Ricky seems the man poised to lead us to the musical promised land. As the end of the millennium nears, a wave of change is evident in the record business, and the executives at

Sony believe their Latin stars will lead the way into the new century.

"I have no crystal ball, but my gut tells me that Latin music can be the next big reservoir of talent for mainstream superstars," says Sony Music chief Tommy Mottola, who was also responsible for grooming Mariah Carey into the hit-producing singer she is today. Mattola is so convinced that Latin music is the next windfall that sources say he's earmarked upward of $10 million to promote Ricky's English-language album and millions more to hire top-notch producers like Puff Daddy and David Foster to guide Latin pop down the same path taken previously by country and hip-hop music.

The new wave of Latin talent is not your father's lambada, or your brother's macarena, because there's nothing gimmicky about it. Latin sounds and rhythms are as old as music itself. Whereas Nashville is the home of country, Latin's musical home base is Miami, Florida, which, not coincidentally, is where Sony Discos is based, the label that has backed Ricky from the start.

Up to this point, probably the most successful crossover Latin artist is Gloria Estefan, the first to tap into the staggering potential of Latin music. Just consider the raw numbers: more than 400 million people claim Spanish as their first language around the world. In America alone, there are over 30 million people of Hispanic descent, making up well over ten percent of the total population.

Cable tapped into this market years ago, with MTV expanding into Latin America, Central America, and South America since the early 1990s. They also broadcast *MTV en Español* in the United States, which is aimed at a young, bilingual group of consumers that have been largely overlooked until now.

But the success of Gloria Estefan and her husband, Emilio, wasn't made possible simply by Latin followers. Through her music, she reached across the cultural divide and brought in non-Hispanics by the arenaful, which is one reason why, in 1997, sales of Latin music rose twenty-five percent.

Like Ricky, Gloria and her husband Emilio won people over through hard work and infectious music. They began humbly in the 1970s as Miami Sound Machine. They scraped by until Sony offered to sign them in 1981. Again like Ricky, they became successful in Latin America first, with two Spanish-language albums, then broke through with the song "Conga."

The song set the stage for others, including Ricky, to follow, by blending Latin rhythms with dance beats, a sound that appealed to Hispanics and Anglos alike. Believing they had the right formula, the Estefans put up their life savings to help produce their first English language album for Sony, *Primitive Love,* which became the first of a string of multiplatinum albums.

And you really know that Latin is hot when the daddy of all merchandisers, Disney, jumps mightily on the bandwagon. Walt Disney World recently added the Bongos Cuban Café, the Estefans' 550-seat, Cuban-themed restaurant to their Downtown Disney attraction in Florida. The café features an authentic Cuban menu of *croquetas, arroz con frijoles,* and *vaca frita.*

But the Estefans did more than just enjoy their own success; they have actively sought to develop, nurture, and promote other Latin artists, such as Jon Secada, who started out as a songwriter for the Estefans' company. Under their guidance, Secada also became a multi-platinum-album act.

Overall, the Estefans employ over two dozen songwriters and almost as many musicians and producers at their record company and studio. And they're not afraid to look across the border for talent, either, having worked with artists including Thalia, a well-known Mexican *novela* star and singer, and Alejandro Fernandez, one of the country's most famous mariachi performers. Overall, the Estefans' personal music machine has made them multimillionaires, with a net worth of over two hundred million dollars.

Which is why, all over the record industry, labels are suddenly anxious to sign Latin artists, who suddenly seemed ubiquitous. In the middle of Hollywood, a huge head shot of Enrique Iglesias peers from a billboard for the local Spanish-language radio station. Luis Miguel, another Latin pop singer, sold more than twelve million copies of the first two albums in his *Romance* trilogy for Warner Music.

Early in 1998, Sony released *Latin Mix USA,* a kind of primer on who's hot in Latin music right now. In addition to showcasing Ricky's "Maria," the collection featured the likes of the legendary Celia Cruz singing an updated cover of "Guantanamera," and hot new sensation Shakira, singing her hit, "Estoy Aquí." Tito Puente's Blackout Allstars also grooved with "I Like It," which was a crossover hit in the mid 1990s.

The album also featured a selection from former rapper turned mega—movie star Will Smith. It's significant because Smith is one non-Hispanic performer who has successfully adopted the Latin rhythms to his own music.

Another gauge of Latin music's popularity is its domination in dance clubs, not only in America but around the world. While nobody is surprised that clubs in L.A. and Miami predominantly feature Latin songs, it's a bit more surprising to know that it's also the rage in places like London, as well.

Although Ricky Martin has the best vantage point to lead the charge of Latin artists into the next century, he's hardly alone in the vanguard. There are several new, established, and reestablished stars hoping to share the success that seems inevitable. One of the newer artists starting to get some recognition is, ironically enough, another Menudo alumni, Ruben Gomez.

Among Gomez's Menudo highlights was a music video of the song "Situation," which featured Tony winner Lea Salonga. Since leaving the group, Gomez charted a solo career by first transforming himself from a squeaky-clean teenager to a Latin hunk—although even when part of Menudo, he was considered the sexy one of the group. His debut album, released by BMG Records, shows off his sexy side, with cuts like the single "Me Vuelves Loco." Unlike Ricky's, though, Ruben's music has a more definitive rock-and-roll sound; edgier, compared with Ricky's supersleek productions.

But as all Latin singers must, Gomez can whisper out a love ballad, such as "Te No Puedo Olvidarme" ("I Can't Forget You").

"Yes, this is a very romantic, touching song about losing the love of your life," he says. "Musically, this song has a very acoustic country feeling to it. All these elements make this song one of my favorites.''

Like Martin, Gomez has been performing since long before his Menudo days, and in fact released his first solo album, *Una Es Ilusíon*, as a youngster of ten. Taking a cue from another well-known teen idol of the era, Gomez chose for the album's first single a Spanish cover of Donny Osmond's ''Puppy Love.'' However, there's a lot more riding on his current solo efforts.

''Taking this step has been an amazing experience for me,'' admits Gomez, who is following the pattern by establishing himself in places like the Philippines and Latin America before confronting American audiences.

''I look forward to performing before audiences who already know me and those I'll soon know, to introduce them to my work as a solo artist,'' he says.

As mentioned previously, some other ex-Menudo boys-to-men, Johnny Lozada, Charlie Masso, Miguel Cancel, Ricky Melendez, Rene Farraet, and Ray Reyes, reunited for the El Reencuentro tour.

When he's not reliving past glories, Johnny Lozada is part of the popular Latin American duo Johnny and Tatiana. But Tatiana does admit that there are some drawbacks to having a former teen idol as a partner.

''The girls love Johnny, and some of them are very jealous,'' she notes. ''Sometimes they bang their hands on the car, and sometimes they throw gum in my hair.''

And speaking of Menudo, amazingly, the group was still making music, although it was now called MDO and had only four members. Their *Un Poco Más* release had been well received, although the days of fan hysteria seemed to be long gone.

If 1998 was considered the year of the woman in the record industry, then 1999 may be the year of the Latin. In addition to Ricky's release, Sony is also hyping discs by Marc Anthony, actress-turned-singer Jennifer Lopez, and perhaps the hottest property, Shakira, who hails from Colombia. To all concerned, it just seems that the planets are aligned just right.

"Lots of different cultures are accepting Latin music," says Julio Vergara, program director of WSKQ, New York's leading Spanish-language radio station.

Marc Anthony, who is probably best known for his stage work in New York, including the ill-fated Paul Simon effort, *Capeman,* says his album is more pop than the dance sounds usually associated with Latin music. While a planned duet with Madonna—another performer who nurtures Latin talent—will help improve his profile to a mass audience, Anthony believes there's still a way to go before Latin music is considered mainstream.

"When I go into stores in Times Square and ask for my album, they say it's in the back, in the International section," Anthony comments. "I recorded it on Forty-seventh Street! How can you get more local than that?"

Shakira hopes her next album, produced by Emilio Estefan, will "demonstrate to the rest of the world that Latin people also can make good pop and good rock."

With so many performers vying for audiences' affection, you might suspect a feud or two, but Ricky denies he feels a rivalry with anyone else. "I guess that we all are in the same boat and for the same reason—to take good music to all that like it. To Ricky Martin his rival is only Ricky Martin."

And of the younger performers, Ricky says he's most

drawn to Shakira. "I admire her voice, music, beauty, and authenticity. And I also admire Julio Iglesias, because he knew how to break the idiomatic boundaries."

Jennifer Lopez has two things going for her to help her break some boundaries. One, she is romantically linked to Sony chief Tommy Mottola, who will make sure her records get airplay, and second, she is already a familiar and liked face, thanks to her numerous film roles, including the title role in *Selena*. Her album is produced by Puff Daddy and, according to Lopez, is "a mix of urban and Latin influences, stuff that makes me dance."

What's incredibly bittersweet in this current explosion of, and interest in, Latin music, is that much of it can be traced back to the singer whose life was cut brutally short just as her career was ready to blast into mainstream America. In 1995, Selena Quintanilla-Perez was considered one of the most promising singers in the Latin world. Called the queen of Tejano—a lively blend of Tex-Mex, pop, country, and German polka, of all things—this style of music was going to be her ticket to international stardom.

She had already been awarded a Grammy and sold three million records, as she readied herself for crossover exposure. Born and raised in Corpus Christi, Texas, Selena and her husband chose to live in the same neighborhood where she had been raised, next door to her parents.

"Selena accepted herself for exactly who she was," says Gregory Nava, who directed *Selena*. "And that's why the Latino community embraced her so much."

Once she had established herself within the Latin community, Selena, whose primary language was English and who had to learn Spanish to sing the songs, planned to expand into mainstream pop with the release of an English language album. But she never got the chance.

On March 31, 1995, the former president of Selena's fan club, Yolanda Salivar, shot the singer to death at a Days Inn motel in Corpus Christi. Selena had gone to meet with Salivar, who was suspected of embezzling from the fan club. Eyewitnesses reported that shortly after going into room 158, Selena had run out, calling for help. As she ran, Salivar, who claimed she'd actually been trying to commit suicide, shot Selena in the back, killing her. Selena had just turned twenty-four years old, and the Latin world mourned, with over 300,000 fans attending her memorial service.

The outpouring of grief was the first indication of just how deeply Selena had touched her audience. And it was bittersweet irony for her family that after her death, Selena found the stardom she had dreamed of in life. Her English album, *Dreaming of You*, debuted at number one on the *Billboard* pop album chart, the first time a Latina had ever achieved the honor.

In a way, the success of the current crop of upcoming Latin stars owes a debt to Selena. "I always say Gloria Estefan left the door ajar for Hispanic artists," says EMI Latin president José Behar. "But it was Selena who blew it wide open."

Thanks to Selena, Gloria, Julio, and all the others who came before him, Ricky was ready to rumba through that door and salsa into the hearts of Americans from coast to coast. And he was about to be given a golden stage upon which to introduce himself.

14

The Grammys

Because he travels so much, Ricky looks forward to coming home to peace and tranquillity. So he was especially upset in late October of 1998 when Hurricane Georges cut a swath of destruction through the Caribbean, including Puerto Rico, a terrifying experience for Ricky's family and friends on the island.

"I *hate* it! It tore up Puerto Rico. The whole area actually. It makes you mad, 'cause you can't do anything; you're powerless against the force of nature. Actually the people of Puerto Rico have been lucky. We belong to the United States, and they'll make sure we're up and running again soon and that things are being repaired."

When asked about the aftermath, he said, "I thought my house would be flooded!" Fortunately, though, it wasn't. However, in many places electricity was out for close to a week, but, as Ricky pointed out, Puerto Rico was much better off than some other islands.

"In the Dominican Republic, Haiti, and Cuba, for instance, the people don't have anything. And at least no one was killed in Puerto Rico. In the Dominican Republic twenty-eight people were killed, and in Cuba even more than one hundred. That's awful; it really is."

Ricky was doubly blessed to come out of Georges unscathed. Not only was his home in Puerto Rico spared, but so was his Miami retreat.

"In my backyard there is a bay; it's really beautiful there," he explained. "But I was afraid that my living room would turn into a bay as well! Fortunately it turned out all right in the end. I live on a small island that's connected to the mainland by bridges. All my neighbors were evacuated, but the hurricane was only going at ninety kilometers an hour when it hit us, and that's nothing compared to the two hundred kph in the beginning."

Ricky and the other Florida residents said a prayer of thanks that the damage had been as minimal as it was. The head of the National Hurricane Center was equally thankful, admitting that the hurricane had fooled them. "We will never know how close we came to a comparable, Hurricane Mitch–like disaster in Key West. We predicted Georges would be a category-three hurricane. It hit land as a two, but it could just as easily have been a category four."

So thanks to the mysterious ways of storms and some good luck, Ricky's South Beach hideaway was left unscathed. And in recent times he has retreated to his home for overdue rest and recuperation, after experiencing another bout of near-exhaustion, which he typically downplayed.

"Oh, but that was nothing! I didn't collapse or anything, but," he admitted, "I had done a couple of countries in one day again and I was just tired out. But by now I know how far I can push myself. I told the record company that after every fifteen days I want a couple of days off.''

At the same time, Ricky didn't want it to appear that he was slowing down. ''Look, visiting four countries in three days is something I'll keep doing because I love doing it. But it mustn't go on for too long. From now on I'll do it for fifteen days in a row, and then I may have five days off.

''For the past two years there has been a lot of traveling, different countries, different cultures, a lot of music obviously. I'm taking a couple of days off now to recharge. I need to be alone; I need to spend some time with myself. I've said this before—I need to connect heart and mind so I can . . . put it this way, in order for me to be honest next time I walk onstage. It's necessary; it's healthy.''

On that kind of schedule, Martin says, ''If it's possible I'll fly home. And then I'll wash my car, play with the dog, and hang out with my friends. You know how I am with friends—they mean everything to me. I take a little breather and step out of that role of Ricky the star, and after five days I just step back into it again. It's much more healthy that way.''

Ricky needed to be at peak form because if it was possible, he was in greater demand than ever, thanks to the tremendous success of *Vuelve*, which had sold over six million copies worldwide.

''It's the same wherever I go,'' he said. ''When you have soul and you feel the rhythm, when the drums are beating, you simply must start dancing. You don't have to understand a word of what's being sung. The important thing is the feeling for the music. The only thing that's different is the sort of music.

"In Latin America, Spain, or Brazil, people love the salsa. Most Europeans, especially Germans, want faster and heavier beats. The only important thing for me is that you can have fun with the music. That's what I'm trying with the new album *Vuelve*."

Martin said *Vuelve* was a departure for him in some ways. "Unlike my earlier style, there are some slow numbers in this album," he noted. "I think I have evolved over the years. In this album, I've used some of the unique sounds that I've picked up from different continents. The sounds, the rhythms, are very earthy. But I will not change the base—it is very Puerto Rican. I don't want to change that, not even for the next album I am working on."

One had to wonder, though, if he was getting tired yet of performing "Maria," which seemed to have eternal life, and might prefer to sing some other songs instead. Ricky was emphatic. "I *love* 'Maria.' Each song is like a little baby that's still growing. And nobody compares one baby to another, right? Each song has its own soul and individuality. That's why I'll always love singing 'Maria.' Yet it's a challenge to write another hit, of course. But I don't let it get to me. Take it easy—that's a cool motto!"

But Ricky had written a song to match the importance of "Maria," as "Copa de la Vida" had proven. And it was on the strength of that tune that Ricky found himself nominated for a Grammy. But even more thrilling was the added invitation to perform at the award ceremonies—a telecast that would be seen by an estimated 200 million people worldwide. It was such an honor that Ricky's promoter, Angelo Medina, felt the need to make an official response.

"For Ricky Martin, it is a commitment and another opportunity to continue promoting the Hispanic culture," Medina said.

The big question for Ricky was which song he should sing. "La Copa de la Vida" had become one of his signature songs around the globe, but "Living la Vida Loca" was a single planned for the new English-language album. Or he could do a medley of both. In the end, Ricky decided to sing in Spanish, since "La Copa de la Vida" was what he'd been nominated for in the Best Latin Pop Performance category, along with fellow nominees Chayanne, José Feliciano, Juan Gabriel, and Enrique Iglesias.

Prior to the awards show, the *L.A. Times* went on the record as saying:

> *Martin should have no difficulty taking home a Grammy. His album* Vuelve *showed that you can craft a million-selling pop masterpiece without insulting your listeners' intelligence.*

In addition, Ricky was also nominated for two 1999 ACE Awards, which recognize outstanding Latin American artists. His album *Vuelve* was nominated for Record and Album of the Year, and he was also up for Male Artist of the Year.

It was almost an embarrassment of riches. But more wealth was on the way.

The Grammys were held on Wednesday, February 24, 1999, at the Shrine Auditorium in downtown Los Angeles, and nearly anyone of importance in the music industry was there. The nontelevised portion of the ceremonies began early in the afternoon, in order to accommodate the numerous awards to be handed out. Then at five o'clock Pacific time, the televised portion began. Scheduled to appear as either presenters or performers on the telecast were a virtual music industry Who's Who, including Celine Dion, Lauryn Hill, Whitney Houston, Madonna, Mariah Carey, Shania Twain, the Dixie Chicks, and Will Smith.

While 1998 may be remembered as the year of the woman, with Madonna and Lauryn Hill leading the pack, the 1999 Grammys will be remembered as Ricky's grand coming-out party. The telecast featured some polished performances, including that of Madonna, who was performing for the first time ever at a Grammy award show, and was hosted ably enough by Rosie O'Donnell. But the evening was plodding along as a typical award presentation until Ricky Martin took the stage and quite simply blew the audience away with his energetic, vibrant rendition of "La Copa de la Vida."

For the first time, the audience seemed to be completely focused on a performance, finding themselves moving in their seats. When the song finished, a breathless Martin looked on in stunned amazement as the audience jumped to its feet, applauding wildly. Ricky had received hundreds of standing ovations before, but this was special because it came from an audience of his peers.

"To get the acceptance of an audience is fascinating, and to see Will Smith doing the jiggy with my song! It's overwhelming. I guess with all those drums and passion that was flowing onstage it made everybody dance," Ricky said later. "A lot of people asked me, 'Were you nervous?' I was not. I really wanted to do it, and you know, for a little while I was a little antsy, and I said, 'First of all, do yoga before you go onstage, and two, you've been doing this since you were twelve years old; why are you gonna change?'

"I felt like a fish in water, I was in control, I was having the best time, but I don't know if you could tell."

Maybe so, but a few minutes later when his name was announced as the winner of the Best Latin Pop award for his album *Vuelve,* Martin looked stunned and deliriously happy. And when Rosie O'Donnell looked into the camera and told America that Ricky was the cutest thing and she just loved his performance, Martin had been given the ultimate stamp of approval. But whether even Ricky understood the magnitude of the sea change that had just occurred was doubtful.

Of course he knew what it meant on a certain professional level. "And to get a Grammy is awesome and a motivation to do great stuff. A Grammy is, of course, credibility, because it's not only the acceptance of the audience, but it is the acceptance of your peers. It's the respect of people that know about these things. I'm talking about musicians, directors, composers, producers, and when you have that in your head, it's like, 'Hey, people with a lot knowledge of what I do are saying that, OK, he did a great job with this production.'

"That evening was very special, not only because I was nominated but because I was performing, and I was performing not in front of people that admired me but I was performing in front of people that I admired. You know, Sting was there and others, and I would look around and I was like, 'What a rush!' It was so great."

Backstage, Ricky was the unexpected beau of the ball,

and he looked on wide-eyed at being alongside the likes of Madonna, who was holding court with the press.

"I'm a Grammy winner and there's no booze here. What is this?" she joked. Prior to that night, she had never won a single Grammy, and now she had taken home four, including Best Pop Album, for *Ray of Light*, and Best Dance Recording. "The win for Best Pop Album was such a shock. I was still coming down from performing. So I never got the chance to thank everybody I wanted to."

Madonna did, however, get a chance to add her own personal congratulations to Ricky when she impulsively joined Ricky when he was talking to the media and kissed him. "I'm just up here to congratulate him! All I can say is, Watch out," she said to the surprised press corps, then explained teasingly, "I had to sneak up on him. He's *so* cute!"

"I am flattered," Ricky said in response to Madonna's attention. "Just to be applauded by the people, by your peers, by people who are in this business, it's fascinating, it really is. It's very important."

Grammy host Rosie O'Donnell admitted, "I never heard of him before tonight, but I'm enjoying him *sooo* much." And in fact, a representative from her show was among the first to call Ricky's label the next day and request him to appear on her show.

Other performers were also taken by Ricky. When reporters asked country group Dixie Chicks what the greatest thrill of the night was, they answered in unison, "Definitely Ricky Martin!"

And when Will Smith was in the press room, he agreed. "Ricky Martin got everyone hyped up! I want to be able to do what Ricky Martin does onstage!'' he added, trying to wiggle his hips à la Ricky.

But the full impact of his Grammy appearance wouldn't become completely clear until the days and weeks following the telecast. Suddenly everything Ricky had dreamed about achieving in America seemed within his immediate grasp.

15

America's New Pop Star

In its March 15, 1999, issue, *Time* magazine ran a feature called "Spicing the Mix—Latin pop prepares to take on America." The article began with the following observation:

> *A funny thing happened last week in Salt Lake City, Utah. After Ricky Martin's electrifying rendition of "La Copa de la Vida" performed the musical equivalent of CPR on a listless Grammy Awards telecast in Los Angeles, fans descended on Salt Lake's record stores and picked them clean of the Latin singer's albums. Runs on his albums were reported in L.A. and Miami too, but none was more surprising than the one in Salt Lake, a town better known for its allegiance to the Osmond Brothers than its enthusiasm for Latin pop.*

What was intriguing about it was that the same phenomenon was being reported all around the country. One employee of Tower Records in Los Angeles noted,

"Women saw how good-looking he was, and that translated to record sales. It always does." L.A.'s Virgin Megastore also sold out the day after the Grammys, and the same scenario was repeated in most major cities.

Vuelve was given a sharp boost and was enjoying its number eleven berth on *Billboard*'s Latin 50 chart, and was the third-best-selling CD on Amazon.com. As *Newsday* summed up:

> *Three minutes and 51 seconds. That's how long it took—from first note to last—for 26-year-old Ricky Martin to become a North American superstar. His extraordinary rendition of "La Copa de la Vida" from his* Vuelve *album on the recent 41st Annual Grammy Awards not only awoke the somnolent, star-studded crowd, but brought it roaring to its feet. In what was the best single-song performance since Michael Jackson introduced the moonwalk while singing "Billie Jean" on the Motown 25th anniversary show more than 15 years ago, Martin, a Puerto Rican, ignited a storm of media attention.*

Perhaps more than anyone, Ricky's manager, Angelo Medina, understood the importance of what had transpired. "Most definitely, this event will change both of our professional lives forever. From now on it will be *before* and *after* the Grammy."

The same night he won the Grammy, Ricky was scheduled to leave on a flight to San Remo, Italy, for a concert. But Sony boss Tommy Mottola was so anxious to have Ricky stay and enjoy the afterparty that he gave Ricky the OK to miss his commercial flight, and instead a Sony corporate jet would fly him out later that night.

"Before boarding the plane," Medina recalls, "Ricky was telling me that everything that happened still seemed like a dream. That it seemed like he had seen it on television and that it hadn't happened to him."

But it had happened, and more than just Ricky would ultimately benefit, the manager believed.

"The mere act of presenting a Latin music award during the live broadcast is a giant step. This is good for Ricky because it will be easier to get more interviews for him on major talk shows in the United States, which we need in order to promote his first English album."

Although many music critics had predicted Ricky would win the award, Medina said he took nothing for granted and was actually relieved it turned out the way it did.

"I'm very happy that Ricky won; if not, it would have been like a cold bath after his successful performance. Ricky will change music. His entrance into the world of English music will cause great changes."

Ricky could not have timed the media glare at a more perfect time. His English-language album, produced by Emilio Estefan Jr., Desmond Child, and Robi Rosa, was scheduled to be released in May 1999, followed by a summer concert tour.

"It's something that I've always wanted to do," he said of his English-language album. "Even when I was recording in Spanish, I was working on this for two and a half years now. We're ready. You know, it was not six months ago, it's not ten months from now, it's *now* when I have to release it, because I guess I'm hungry for it."

As a result of the new interest in Ricky, the release of his first single off the album, "Living la Vida Loca" ("Living the Crazy Life") began getting radio airplay within weeks after the Grammys, and fans were effusive, filling the Internet singing their own praises of Ricky and his song.

> *Ricky Martin is the hottest guy in the world!!!!!!!!!!!!!!!! Ricky Martin is the finest guy in the whole world. I have liked him since he was in Menudo, in the movie* Salsa, *and on* General Hospital. *I love Ricky Martin. His new song "Livin' la Vida Loca" is the best video. I love you, Ricky!!!!!!!!!*
>
> *ABSOLUTELY FABULOUS!!!!!*
>
> *I don't really listen to Latin music that much, but Ricky Martin's music has really caught my attention. When my three-year-old hears the song on the radio in the car, she tells me, "Mommy, it's time to shake!"*
>
> *Hey, Ricky Martin is soooooooo hot in his new video "Livin' la Vida Loca." This song is a GREAT song. This song makes me wanna get up and sing! You are soooooooo hot, Ricky!!!!*
>
> *"Livin' la Vida Loca" has to be THE best Latin song I have ever heard. It's awesome. I can't wait until the CD single is out. I think "Livin' la Vida Loca" is the hottest song by Ricky Martin. I have*

also seen the music video and it's even hotter than the song itself.

Even though he had very little free time, Ricky says he does go on the Internet occasionally. "You know, they send messages, and the best part is answering them. 'Oh, I don't believe he wrote to me; can you please tell me who did that?' you know? So it's like, maybe you won't believe me, but yes, it's me, I swear." And although some celebrities find fan pages unnerving, Ricky is flattered. "I don't mind at all."

Interestingly, though, Ricky's favorite song on the album isn't "Living la Vida Loca," but "I Am Made of You." "Without a doubt. 'I Am Made of You' is when I met with my higher power today," says Martin, who is a practicing Buddhist. "You know, it starts with, 'I came a long way from out of nowhere. I stand before you all alone, like a wolf's cry in the distance; I heard the calling of your soul,' and I just came back from India and I had all sorts of these spiritual awakenings because you have to be in touch with yourself in order to be able to deal with everything.

"Even if you're not in this business you have to be in touch with yourself, because of what society's like nowadays. I'm not being pessimistic, just realistic, so . . . this thing of God, Buddha, Allah, however you want to call it, we have to keep it simple. That song is very special for me."

Even though Ricky's label had released the single, the album was still a work in progress, with the title still undetermined as of March 1999. Among the possibilities were *Spanish Eyes, Private Emotion, Around the World in a Day,* and *Ricky Martin.*

"The only issue about it being called *Ricky Martin,*" he pointed out, "is my first album was also called *Ricky Martin.* I like *Spanish Eyes* because it has an essence, is very energetic, and definitely has romanticism. But the good part about everything is that it can be called *Spanish Eyes* in Australia, *Private Emotion* in Europe, and *Ricky Martin* in America."

As for the album itself, Ricky says, "I'm presenting myself as who I am. I cannot wear a mask to go onstage, so I have infusion from Ska to Latin to sounds of the sixties. I have balance, classic ballads, more edgy ballads; still, it's not a salad."

Although the album was originally intended to have twelve songs, Ricky's newest best friend, Madonna, forced a change of plans when she approached Ricky about doing a duet.

"You know, she showed up in the press conference saying, you know, 'I'm sorry, guys, but I have to congratulate him,' you know, and she came and kissed me, and ever since I've been working with her. I met her before the Grammys—we've been able to work in different TV shows in Europe, and that was great. But ever since, we've been locked in the studio dealing and creating, and it's been fascinating to work with someone so talented, so smart. She's a legend; she's a living legend. I respect her music; I respect her work.

"She's so into changing culture; she always has been. She enjoys the Latin sounds, she's energetic, I'm energetic, so let's do something!" Martin told *USA Today*'s Jeannie Williams.

Overseeing the collaboration is William Orbit, who also worked with Madonna on *Ray of Light,* her most successful album in years. Although it was a great coup to have a duet with Madonna, Ricky was really more interested in the experience. Even though Ricky had written several songs for himself, the duet would be penned by Madonna.

"I have to work on my language first before I do lyrics. But I give my input. She doesn't want to sound like me; I don't want to sound like her—it's fusion. I also let the producer know where I'm at emotionally: 'This is me, this I like, this I don't like.'

"I promised Madonna that if it works for my album, great. If it works for hers, great. For a soundtrack, great. Or just to have fun, great. I told her, 'Let's not be dealing with a deadline. Let's take it easy.' It has to come out of comfort." Then he adds, "Of course, I'd love for it to be part of my album. Are you kidding?"

Since then, he and Madonna have been close, with Ricky accompanying her to some Oscar festivities in late March, including the annual *Vanity Fair* bash, where guests included Monica Lewinsky. Their closeness immediately prompted speculation of a romance, especially after Ricky revealed he and Rebeca were no longer involved. But from all accounts, it is truly just a close, budding friendship and professional collaboration.

While preparing for the release of his album, Ricky kept busy giving interviews and, as always, performing, taking his *Vuelve* show to Brazil and Mexico—a show that seemed to grow with each album.

"I usually have at least forty people traveling, and out of those forty people, at least fifteen musicians onstage with me. It's very energetic, a lot of dancing, and a lot of romanticism as well. Just what you can feel and sense on the album is what I usually present at my concerts."

After that minitour, Ricky would return to New York to introduce his album in May 1999—an event that drew journalists from all corners of the world.

Sony was sparing no expense to give Ricky the promotional campaign of a lifetime. In addition to booking him on all the top talk shows, they also hired the best photographers for his publicity photos.

"I got to work with Herb Ritts. He's awesome. We did a photo shoot and he gave me his book and everything. It was amazing. Just the fact of being able to exchange ideas with someone like him is really interesting."

Although Ricky can sound star-struck on occasion, in the end, there's not one aspect of his career he doesn't control.

"I have to," he says simply. "My face is the one out there, not only for photo shoots but in my concerts. What you see in my concerts are my ideas. I mean, I can contract people to come in with great ideas, but at the end of the day what I feel comfortable with for me and for my personality, my wardrobe, concerts, my music, is me, definitely."

As Ricky acclimated to his newfound popularity in America, he was able to put it in some perspective, and admitted that while he was pleased, he had also worked for this very thing.

"When you start working in a certain market you have to be positive. When I started I didn't want to be an international artist that is visiting. I want to be part of the country. So tell me, fill me in on what your country is like.'' And that way, he feels, people will be more accepting, regardless of the country.

One of the programs Ricky appeared on was *CNN Worldbeat*—not your typical pop star's forum. But Ricky showed himself to be thoughtful and articulate, and addressed the issue of his music being a form of communication.

''Language is not important at all. It is the sound that is important.''

When asked why he thought Latin music was gaining so markedly in popularity, he smiled and suggested, ''Maybe it's because Latin American artists are now willing to go out there.''

Despite being poised as the first great crossover Latin act, Ricky made sure his fans understood that ''I will never stop singing in Spanish. But this is a communications business, and it's all about getting closer to cultures.''

It was also about taking opportunities when they were presented, and Ricky's cup was running over.

16

Still Ricky

The months between his Grammy performance and the release of his album were a blur of activity for Ricky. It would be difficult to believe that any performer who didn't have Ricky's fifteen years of experience would have been completely overwhelmed by the intensity of expectation and the glare of attention brought about by a 470 percent increase in album sales since the night he brought the house down at the Grammys. But for Ricky, it was business as usual.

Every day seemingly offered a new adventure. One day he was recording the song "Come to Me" for his album with Turkish singer Sertab Erener, and the next day he was appearing in a benefit for the Rain Forest Foundation, founded ten years ago by Sting and Trudie Styler. Ricky joined regulars Elton John, Sting, and James Taylor, as well as special guests Charles Aznavour, Tony Bennett, Sandra Bernhard, Don Henley, and Billy Joel in preparing to appear alongside Luciano Pavarotti in Italy over the summer.

If the first time hearing his own song on the radio made

Ricky cry, seeing his video for "Living la Vida Loca" might have made him blush. While singing the lyric, "She'll make you take your clothes off and go dancing in the rain," he is having hot candle wax dripped on his bare chest.

"You have to see it twice!" he says. "It's a lot of information. It goes from a club to a funky, cheap hotel, to walking in the middle of the city with lots of dancers, lots of stunts—even a car crashing."

Ricky says that the scene happened by accident because, while doing a take, he jokingly told the actress to pour the wax on him. But the director liked it so much, he insisted it stay in the video.

The biggest irony is that the man who gyrates to "Living la Vida Loca," seems to be on a quest to find inner peace and tranquillity. Never a party animal—"I'm not too much into cocktails and parties and blah-blah-blah"—Ricky is more concerned with his spiritual self. "I have to go back to India, Nepal, Tibet," he says, revealing that he plans to spend New Year's Eve of 1999 in the Himalayas.

He's drawn to that part of the world, he says, because he wants "to be grounded and focused. In this business you deal with so much fantasy, the adrenaline is constantly going. I've got to have twenty to forty minutes a day to myself and ask myself how I'm affecting others, how I'm letting others affect me and not be harmed."

Ricky also finds Indian music very healing and soothing, and says, "I would love to capture the rich sounds of India. I'm very interested in bhangra. And I've been listening to Zakir Hussain. *Sounds of the Desert* is very impressive. I'd be honored to work with him sometime in the future.''

Again, Ricky keeps proving he's not the average pop star and teen idol.

As the release date of his album neared, the pieces were falling into place. The CD would be in stores on May 11 and contain fourteen songs, including a ''Spanglish'' remix of ''Maria'' and an English cover of ''La Copa de la Vida,'' with the album to be titled *Ricky Martin.* Not counting Madonna's fees, the album had cost more than a million dollars to produce, but Sony believed they would make back ten times that much or more.

The label planned to make an initial shipment of five million copies, with three million for international distribution and two million for American consumers. In addition to ''Living la Vida Loca'' and the remixes, the album contains Ricky's usual mix of song styles.

''Be Careful with My Heart,'' his much anticipated duet with Madonna, is sung mostly in English but has some Spanish thrown in as well. And Ricky sang another duet, ''Private Emotions,'' with Swedish singer Maya, who Sony hopes will become their next crossover performer. ''Shake Your Bom Bom,'' produced by Emilio Estefan, and ''Spanish Eyes'' are both danceable tunes. But Ricky goes for a different emotion completely with ''She's All that I Ever Had'' (also called ''Bella''), which he dedicates to his grandmother.

The only thing left to do was wait and see if all the promise was fulfilled. But regardless of how the American public would ultimately receive him, Ricky would accept it with the same grace and humility he had shown during his entire career, for which, he has said repeatedly, he's in for the long haul.

Even though at some point in the future he'd like to work in film behind the camera and try his hand at writing, "being onstage is not something I want to let go of—the feeling of control and to be yourself. It doesn't matter what you do onstage; it's art. Yes, you will be judged, but you will also be forgiven if something goes wrong. Definitely I have to be onstage.

"But I'd also like to do something behind the camera. I've learned a lot from a lot of directors I've worked with over the years. And maybe I'll stop for a couple of years and study cinematography; then maybe I can start directing my own videos. That's something I'd love to try, because it's another perspective."

Perhaps most important to Ricky, however, is the legacy he will leave as a human being.

"I'd like to be remembered as someone who taught others about Latin cultures. Someone who worked a lot. Someone to trust. And at the same time, someone who was always grounded. In this business it could get crazy because you are constantly looking for acceptance, and the acceptance of an audience is applause, and the applause is people telling you how good you are. But at the same time, when a lot of people are telling you you're great, it can get you a little messed up if you aren't in control or in touch with yourself. If you're not spiritually solid.

"I want to stay the same and in twenty years go back to that little kid that would ride his bike in the neighborhood and ask him, 'Hey, are you proud of who you've become?' "

There seems little doubt what the answer will be.

Ricky Fast Facts

Full name: Enrique Martin Morales
Zodiac sign: Capricorn
Height: 6′1″
Weight: 165 lbs.
Eyes: Brown
Hair: Light brown
Father: Enrique Martin Negroni
Mother: Nerieda Morales
Siblings: Fernando, Angel, Eric, Daniel, and Vanessa
Irrational fear: Snakes
Believes his best quality is: Sincerity
Believes his worst quality is: Sincerity
Hobby: Collects matchbooks from all over the world

These Are a Few of His Favorite Things:

Foods:

Chinese
Cuban
Italian
Japanese
Mexican
(Least favorite—Seafood)

Fashion Designers:

Dolce & Gabbana
Giorgio Armani
Helmut Lang
Paul Smith
Yohji Yamamoto

Vacation Spots:

Puerto Rico
Key West, Florida
Rio de Janeiro
Seychelles islands
Grand Canyon, Arizona

Music:

Brazilian
Classic rock
Classical
New Age
Salsa

Movies:

Fresa y Chocolate
Il Postino
Law of Desire
Platoon
The Godfather

Favorite Actor:

Robert De Niro

Songs:

"Faithfully" (Journey)
"Fragile" (Sting)
"Fuego de Noche, Nieve de Día" (Ricky Martin)
"The Man I'll Never Be" (Boston)

Favorite Singer:

Miguel Bose

Poetry:

Angel Morales
Arthur Rimbaud
Garcia Lorca
Mario Benedetti
T.S. Eliot

Books:

La Tregua (Mario Benedetti)
The Seven Spiritual Laws of Success: A Practical Guide to the Fulfillment of Your Dreams (Deepak Chopra)
Human Dilemma (Iraida Negroni, Ricky's grandmother)
One Hundred Years of Solitude (Gabriel García Márquez)
Confidential Clerk (T.S. Eliot)

Ricky on the 'Net

Australia's First Ricky Martin Site:
http://www.dot.net.au/~austv/ricky.html

Katja's Ricky Page:
http://www.geocities.com/SunsetStrip/Pit/5541/

Ricky Martin East Coast Style:
http://www.geocities.com/SunsetStrip/Lounge/4695/links.htm

Milagros's Ricky Info Site:
http://www.geocities.com/SunsetStrip/Lounge/4695/links.htm

Asian Friends of Ricky Martin:
http://www.home.talkcity.com/BasinSt/rizza3

Rosaline's Ricky Martin Zone:
http://www.geocities.com/SouthBeach/Bluffs/1472

La Bomba and WebFather's Ricky Martin Page:
http://www.dot.net.au/~austv/ricky.html

Rediff on the Net:
http://www.rediff.com/style/1998/jun/20ricky.htm

Ricky Martin Net:
http://www.aquaspa.com/ricky/default.htm

Menudo 2MDO:
http://www.geocities.com/~menudo2mdo/

Ricky Martin Official Site:
http://www.rickymartin.com

Jaidee's Ricky Martin World:
http://www.geocities.com/SunsetStrip/balcony/2811

Gia's Hideaway:
http://www.geocities.com/EnchantedForest/Tower/5639

The Hot Window of Ricky:
http://www.geocities.com/EnchantedForest/Tower/5639

The Unofficial Ricky Martin Homepage:
http://www.members.tripod.com/~SharonS/
RickyMartin.html

Vuelva:
http://www.rickymartinvuelve.com

Gaby's Ricky Page:
http://www.members.tripod.com/~Andy_Gaby/
RickyMartin.html

R M International Fanclub:
http://www.rickymartin.coqui.net

Miguel Morez Guardian Angels:
http://www.members.tripod.com/~MMGA

Ricky's Memorabilia Page:
http://www.members.aol.com/CColey0815/index.html

Menudo:
http://www.robt.simplenet.com/menudo/men.html

Marika's Ricky Martin Page:
http://www.mars.arts.u-szeged.hu/~dfun/ericky.html

Ricky Martin en Puerto Rico:
http://www.endi.com/proyectos/rickymartin/HTML/canciones.html

Ricky Martin y Más International Fan Club:
http://www.members.aol.com/Gana13/rmymi.html

Ricky Martin L.A. Connection:
http://www.rmlac.com

The Ricky Martin World:
http://www.geocities.com/SunsetStrip/Palladium/7235

La Sala de Ricky Martin—Ricky Martin's World:
http://www.members.xoom.com/vuelve

The Ricky Martin World:
http://www.angelfire.com/ar/RICKYMARTIN/

UBL: Artist Ricky Martin:
http://www.ubl.com/ubl/cards/017/8/44.html

Ricky Martin: the Man:
http://www.careweb.com/ricky/disco.htm

Ricky Martin Rendez-Vous:
http://www.geocities.com/Hollywood/Screen/6609/Welcome.html

Raul Roa's Webpage:
http://www.home1.gte.net/raulroa/intropage.html

Spanish-Language Sites:

Ricky Martin-El Mundo Está de Pie:
http://www.vistamagazine.com/marrick.htm

Trabajo:
http://www.aquaspa.com/ricky/es/trabajo/

Penta Music, Ricky Martin:
http://www.inetcorp.net.mx/PENTA/martin~1.htm

Lauren Films:
http://www.laurenfilm.es/lauren98/films/film010.htm

Ricky Martin in Korea:
http://www.lamusica.com/rickymartinkorea.htm

Organización Zeppelin:
http://www.mexplaza.udg.mx/zeppelin/historiazepp.html

Cantantes Latinos:
http://www.estb.baleares.net/pagtarde/ANLOPEZ.HTM

Teletipo Europa Press:
http://www.noticias.ole.es/teletipo/1999/01/14/19990114140234-CUL-SUC.html

La ACE Anuncia Sus Nominaciones:
http://www.nuevamerica.com/ace/

Retila Magazine Contents:
http://www.retila.com/retila12/topten.html

Grupos y Artistas: Noticias:
http://www.gruposyartistas.com/pop/reencuentro/noticias.htm

Additional Spanish-language Sites:

http://www.pegasus.cul.mx/~95170683/Principal.html

http://www.nalejandria.com.ar/01/bialik/h/bialik98/yael.htm

http://www.rtve.es/tve/programo/avan3/tv3s0101.htm

http://www.fortunecity.com/boozers/crownanchor/437/ricky.html

Filmography

Television:

1992 *Alcanzar una Estrella II* (*Reach for a Star*)
1993 *Getting By*
1994–96 *General Hospital*
1995 *Barefoot in Paradise* (Pilot for ABC)

Theater:

1991 *Mama Ama el Rock (Mom Loves Rock)*
1996 *Les Misérables*

Discography

In addition to providing a general overview of Ricky's musical body of work, this section also includes the song titles for each album, as well as Internet sites where you can find the albums for sale.

Overview

Solo Albums:

Ricky Martin (1991, Sony)
Me Amarás (1993, Sony)
A Medio Vivir (1995, Sony)
Vuelve (1998, Sony)

Singles of Note:

"Maria" remixes (1997, Sony)
"The Cup of Life" (1998, Sony) *Official song of the 1998 World Cup*
"La Bomba" remixes (1998, Sony)

Multiple Artist Albums:

Hey Jude—Tributo a Los Beatles (1995, Sony)
Eres—Sexta Entrega de Premios Eres (1996, Fonovisa)

Paul Anka—Amigos (1996, Sony)
Voces Unidas (1996, EMI Latin) *Atlanta 1996 Olympics*
Allez! Ola! Ole!—Music of the World Cup (1998, Columbia) *Official World Cup album*
Hercules Soundtrack (1997, Walt Disney Records) *Spanish-language release*
Latin Mix USA (1999, Sony/Columbia)

Additional Compilations:

Feliz Navidad Te Desean
Gigantes de la Canción
Navidad en las Americas

Where to find Ricky Martin music on the Internet:

http://www.cdnow.com
http://www.soundstone.com
http://www.latincd.com (also has Menudo)

Ricky Martin!

Song Titles:

1. Fuego contra Fuego
2. Dime que Me Quieres
3. Corazón entre Nubes
4. Ser Feliz
5. Susana
6. Conmigo Nadie Puede
7. Vuelo
8. El Amor de Mi Vida

9. Te Voy a Conquistar
10. Popotitos
11. Juego de Ajedrez

Me Amarás

Song Titles:

1. No Me Pidas Más
2. Es Mejor Decrise Adíos
3. Entre el Amor y los Halagos
4. Lo que Nos Pase, Pasará
5. Elle Es
6. Me Amarás
7. Ayúdame
8. Eres Como el Aire
9. Qué Día es Hoy
10. Hooray! Hooray! (It's a Holiday)

A Medio Vivir

Song Titles:

1. Fuego de Noche, Nieve de Día
2. A Medio Vivir
3. Maria
4. Te Extraño, Te Olvido, Te Amo
5. Dónde Estarás
6. Volverás
7. Revolución
8. Somos la Semilla
9. Como Decrite Adiós
10. Bon Bon de Azúcar

11. Corazón
12. Nada es Imposible

Vuelve

Song Titles:

1. La Copa de la Vida
2. Vuelve
3. Por Arriba, por Abajo
4. Lola, Lola
5. Casi un Bolero
6. Corazonado
7. La Bomba
8. Hagamos el Amor
9. Perdido Sin Tí
10. Así Es la Vida
11. Marcia Baila
12. No Importa la Distancia
13. Gracias por Pensar en Mí

About The Author

Kathleen Tracy is an entertainment journalist and the author of numerous biographies and film and television companions, including *Don Imus: America's Cowboy*, *The Boy Who Would Be King*, *The Complete Jackie Chan Handbook*, *This Girl's Got Bite: A Guide to Buffy's World* and *Ellen*. She lives in Sherman Oaks, CA.